THE
FATAL
FLAW

THE FATAL FLAW

At The Heart of Religious Liberalism

DUNCAN HOWLETT

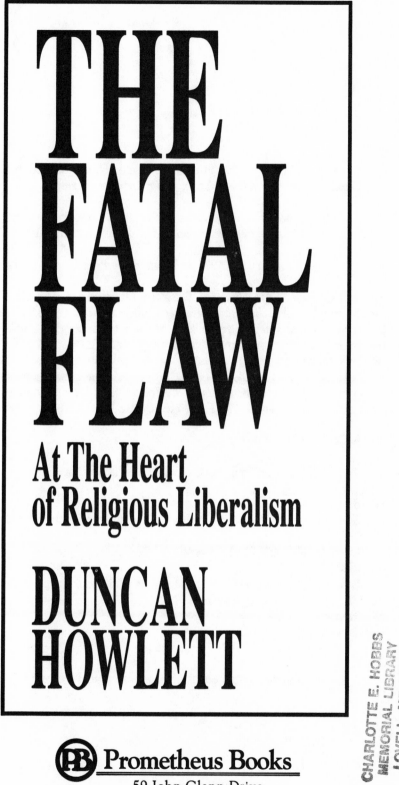

Prometheus Books

59 John Glenn Drive
Amherst, New York 14228-2197

The portion of the poem that appears on page 169 is from Edith Sitwell, *The Canticle of the Rose* (New York: Vanguard Press, 1949).

The portion of "Johnny Appleseed's Hymn" that appears on page 191 is from Vachel Lindsay, *Collected Poems* (Macmillan Company, 1925).

Published 1995 by Prometheus Books

99 98 97 96 95   5 4 3 2 1

Library of Congress Cataloging-in-Publication Data

Howlett, Duncan.
    The fatal flaw at the heart of religious liberalism / Duncan Howlett.
        p.   cm.
    Includes bibliographical references and index.
    ISBN 0-87975-923-2
    1. Liberalism (Religion)—Christianity. 2. Faith and reason—Christianity. 3. Christianity—Forecasting. I. Title.
BR1615.H68   1994
230'.046—dc20   94-26944
                                                                          CIP

Printed in the United States of America on acid-free paper.

To
Melvin Arnold
in gratitude

Contents

Preface

Back of this book lie three others, written over a long period of time. First, *Man Against the Church: The Struggle of Religion with Ecclesiasticism* (Beacon, 1954) grew out of the introduction to a much longer undertaking, which traced the development of Liberalism in religion from ancient Greece to the present day, and was the substance of a course I taught at the Crane Theological School at Tufts University.

Second, *The Fourth American Faith* (Harper & Row, 1964) attempted to delineate Liberalism in religion as the new faith that Protestant, Catholic, and Jewish leaders were becoming concerned about in the 1950s. They saw the movement as a threat to the three "established" faiths, and called it variously "secularism," "agnosticism," and the "religion of democracy." What they saw was not a fourth but a second faith, since, in its principles, it stood over against the traditional views of religion shared by the other three.

Third, *The Critical Way in Religion* (Prometheus, 1980) attempted to spell out in detail the beliefs of religious Liberals and to show how the movement emerged as an intrinsic part of the culture of the West.

The present book draws on all three of its predecessors and on many lectures as well, among them the Minns Lectures at the Meadville Theological School, University of Chicago affiliate, in 1979; the Essex Hall Lecture at the British General Assembly of Unitarian Churches at Aberdeen, Scotland, 1985; the Dudlean Lecture at Harvard University, 1985; two lecture series at the Unitarian Universalist Congregation, Atlanta, Georgia, 1982 and 1983; two at the Unitarian Universalist Church of Westport, Connecticut, 1983 and 1984; the

9

Davies Memorial Lecture at All Souls Church, Washington, D.C.; the Thaddeus B. Clark Lecture at the Unitarian Universalist Church of St. Louis, Missouri, and many others. The question-and-answer periods following these lectures were of immense value to me in working through the ideas developed in the following pages.

The writing extended over a period of some ten years. In the course of such an undertaking one accumulates indebtedness to more people than it is possible properly to acknowledge. Deserving special mention, however, are Sonja Millett, who typed, retyped, and computerized the several drafts through which the manuscript passed; Thomas Gallie, past chairman of the department of mathematics at Duke University, and Harry Crosby, past chairman of the department of rhetoric at Boston University, both of whom read the manuscript; and finally to Melvin Arnold, former president of Harper & Row, whose acumen, professional expertise, and enthusiasm for the project from the start were crucial in bringing it to completion. Finally, like so many who have been immersed in writing over a long period of time, I gratefully acknowledge the forbearance and unfailing support of Carolyn, my wife and companion for over fifty years.

Center Lovell, Maine
October 1994

Introduction

Who am I? Who are you? What are we? We do not know.

Where did we come from? Where are we going? Why are we here? We do not know those things either.

These are religious questions. Down through the ages, the religions of humanity have been trying to answer them for us. They have told us about gods and devils, angels and spirits of every kind. They have assembled sacred scriptures and developed great theologies, elaborate rituals, and stern moral codes. They have reared great temples to the gods, drawn people to worship and prayer, and often, but not always, looked after the poor and needy as well.

Believing and Questioning

Most of the people most of the time have believed what the religions have taught. Except in the West. In Western culture a tradition of questioning developed. In Greece, some 2,500 years ago, a new nonreligious approach to knowledge and understanding emerged when a small group of men called philosophers began looking at the world around them and explaining what they saw, not as a succession of divine interventions in the human world, but as a natural process of cause and effect.

The observing, questioning attitude toward knowledge proved to be only intermittent at the outset. Nor did it become widespread. However, it was persistent. In the Renaissance, two thousand years later, questioning, observing, and exploring for new knowledge

11

emerged as a powerful and pervasive movement outside, not inside the church. The practice came to full flower in the period we know as the Enlightenment in the sixteenth, seventeenth, and eighteenth centuries in western Europe.

It was not until the nineteenth and twentieth centuries that the idea of questioning official church teachings and of searching out new and better ones gained acceptance within the church. It came at the hands of Liberal Protestant Christians. Dismayed by the clamor of conflicting theologies among and within the religions, the Liberals called for an open examination of the validity of official dogma and a frank reaching out for new and better church teachings. Impressed by the advances then being made in scientific thinking, they tried to introduce scientific standards into the thought patterns of their religion.

In the end the Liberal Protestant Christians called for what amounted to a new paradigm for religion. They felt the need for a nontheocentric thought structure—one that was broad enough not to require belief in a Deity, a Transcendent, or even "Something" on which to rest their religion.

The word *paradigm* as used here was given currency by Thomas Kuhn in his notable book *The Structure of Scientific Revolutions* (1962).[1] Seeking to understand the birth and growth of science, he found the key in the concept paradigm. It was not new with him, as he readily acknowledged. The word had entered the language back in the fifteenth century. What was new was Kuhn's use of it as a means of understanding the nature of science.

Defining the concept precisely, he wrote: "Paradigms are universally recognized scientific achievements that for a time provide model problems and solutions to a community of practitioners." Discovering the role of paradigms in the history of science, he asserted, transformed his understanding of the nature of scientific advance. Scientific research, he concluded, amounts to "a strenuous and devoted attempt to force nature into the conceptual boxes applied by professional education."

In an interview thirty years after *The Structure* was published, Kuhn said: "I sweated blood and blood and blood writing *Structures* and finally I had a breakthrough"—the concept of the paradigm. By the term Kuhn meant an archetypal experiment. Galileo's Tower of Pisa demonstration of the uniform speed of falling objects is an example. "Scientists are deeply conservative," Kuhn observed. "Once indoctrinated into a particular paradigm—a particular way of thinking—they generally devote themselves to solving "problems whose solutions reenforce the paradigm they already hold rather than challenging it."[2]

Religion and Science

Kuhn's concept of the paradigm is basic. It can be applied in any field, not only that of science. The parallel with religion is striking. As with science, each of the great religions developed a pattern of thought that was accepted by a community of professional practitioners. As with science, that pattern thereafter provided model problems and solutions for the community that held them. Kuhn, perceiving the role of the paradigm in the development of scientific thought, gained a sudden and great new understanding of what science is, and how it grew following its inception some 2,500 years ago. Applying the same principle to religion, we are led to a similar enlightening conclusion. Just as prevailing patterns of scientific thought bring about "a strenuous and devoted attempt to force nature into the conceptual boxes supplied by professional education," so to an even greater degree do Christianity, Judaism, and Islam engage in a strenuous and devoted attempt to force their thinking into conceptual boxes supplied by professional theological education.

There are, however, striking differences between religion and science when the concept of the paradigm is applied to them. In religion the problem of shaking loose from the paradigms of the past is compounded by a central, all-pervading concept peculiar to religion alone—that of divine revelation. An integral part of that doctrine is the belief that through revelation the religions hold Truth. The validity of the truth they believe they hold is in turn guaranteed by a source they believe to be divine. They hold that certain privileged mortals—the prophets, seers and illuminaries of the ages—received that Truth at divine hands and passed it on to the rest of us. The task of religion is thereby transmuted from one of discovery—the task of science—to the explanation and interpretation of revelation—the task of religion.

In the established religions, Christianity no less than any other, tradition takes center stage. In religion, you begin with the sacred age-old traditions of ritual and myth, language and story, documents and priesthoods, each sacred in its own way and all of it stable and unchanging at an elementary level. As a result, in religion we do not have a succession of paradigms of the sort Kuhn so brilliantly delineated in the history of science. In religion we have a different paradigm in each sect or group. Each individual paradigm is more or less stable and unchanging. The thought patterns differ from group to group, but all are alike in seeking to maintain down through the centuries the central core of what each believes the Truth to be.

What Is Religion?

Scientists generally agree as to what science is. Religious leaders, on the other hand, do not agree as to what religion is. They understand religion according to the old paradigm which centers on belief in the Divine. In the new paradigm, not belief but questioning and exploring are central. In the new paradigm we are confronted with a new concept of what religion itself is. And so we have first to ask: what is religion?

A superabundance of definitions is available. My file of them, collected over the years, contains more than a hundred. I shall not add to the list with yet another. Reviewing them shows that they fall easily into two major groups. The one, the older, widely accepted, finds the center of religion in belief in God, or a Power or "Something." In this view, if you lack that belief or faith you do not have religion.

Hans Küng, a liberal Catholic theologian, provides us with as good a delineation of the older paradigm as we might find. "Religion," he writes, "always deals with an experiential 'encounter with the holy,' whether this 'sacred reality' be understood as power, as forces (spirits, demons, angels), as (a personal) God, as (an impersonal) Divine, or an ultimate reality (Nirvana). . . . Religion," he concludes, "is a social and individual relationship, vitally realized in a tradition and community (through doctrine, ethos, and generally ritual as well) with something that transcends or encompasses man and his world: with something always to be understood as the utterly final, true reality (the Absolute, God, Nirvana)."[3]

In short, Küng, like almost all religious writers, defines religion in terms of Deity, in one form or another. To pin the point down he adds: "In contrast to philosophy, religion is concerned at once with a message of salvation and the way to salvation."

Küng sees religion in the new paradigm, however, when he concludes with the following: "Religion is a *lived life.* . . . It is a *believing view of life,* an *approach to life,* a *way of life,* and therefore a *fundamental pattern* embracing the individual and society . . . through which a person . . . sees and experiences, thinks and feels, acts and suffers everything. . . . Religion provides a comprehensive meaning for life, guarantees supreme values and unconditional norms, creates a spiritual community and home."[4]

The Merriam Webster Collegiate Dictionary, 9th edition, supports Küng's position. Among the definitions we read: "4. Religion is a cause or principle or system of beliefs held to with ardor and faith."[5] Many a present-day writer corroborates this view, which, of course, is the source of the fourth definition of religion the Merriam people list.

A New Paradigm for Religion

In the new paradigm for religion, the old demand that lies at the heart of the organized religions—that in religion we believe by faith—is missing. In the new paradigm, we are invited to explore more than to believe. In the new paradigm there never comes a point where the pursuit of truth by questioning is replaced by the idea of Truth revealed from on high. In the new paradigm, religion, like every other field of human endeavor, is marked by a healthy respect for our human capacity for error. In religion in the new paradigm, the pursuit of goodness, righteousness, truth, and beauty must meet the same standards of testing and requirements for questing that in Western culture are observed in every other field of human endeavor.

In the new paradigm for religion, doubt, religion's oldest enemy, becomes religion's best friend. Doubt leads to questions; questions lead to answers. Answers reached at the end of a succession of probing questions are answers in which we have confidence. Answers in which we have confidence provide us with the sense of certitude we seek in religion. If the teachings the religious offer have been arrived at by pressing the process of inquiry as far as it will go, then we really believe. We believe because we are genuinely persuaded, not because some ecclesiastical authority has assured us that we can believe if we try, or that we must if we are to be "saved." With the questioning process pressed to its farthest limits, we believe because we can do no other. In the new paradigm for religion, we really believe only when we have probed our way down to fundamentals so basic that, with our human limitations, we can see nothing beneath them.

Religion Among Secular Writers

Today in the West the thrust of independent thinking in religion is felt among so-called secular thinkers far more than among the religious professionals. Right now, at the end of the twentieth century the most original, interesting, and exciting books that deal with basic religious concepts are written not by theologians, but scientists. A. Zee's *Fearful Symmetry* is such a book. So are many of Stephen Jay Gould's, *The Flamingo's Smile* and *Wonderful Life,* for example. Richard Feynman, atomic physicist and Nobel Laureate, always insisted that you don't gain basic knowledge by searching for the profundities of existence. Go at things the other way around, he advised. "Nature is going to come out the way she is. . . . When we go to investigate it we shouldn't pre-decide what it is we are trying to do."[6]

None of these writers, or a hundred more that might come to mind, is a clergy person. The same may be said for uncounted other writers, not scientists in the technical sense, but no less imbued with the Western intellectual tradition. They may or may not use the word *religion* yet they are often religious in the most profound sense of the word. John Rawls's *Political Liberalism,* his introduction in particular, is an example of so-called secular writing that shows great insight into the religious problems of our time.*

---

*See Appendix

The Fatal Flaw and the Great Hope

The Liberals in religion never achieved the goal they sought. Always there came a point where they ceased asking questions, ceased reaching out for new concepts, and returned to the older pattern of belief. This was a fatal flaw, yet they left it untouched at the heart of their movement. The two approaches are mutually contradictory. If inquiry and exploration are appropriate, dogma resting on revelation and the authority of the church has no place in our religious thought structure. If dogma is valid, inquiry is not merely unnecessary, it is impertinent, inappropriate, and not to be tolerated. The failure of the Liberals to eliminate this contradiction from the new thought structure they sought to build ultimately destroyed the movement.

What would happen if religion in the West were now to take the standards of the Western intellectual tradition as its own and set out to meet them? This is the question that emerges in the new paradigm. Contemporary society cannot long continue with a religion that is inconsistent with our basic mindset. The hour is late, and the need is great. We are already on our way. The guideposts are there, set up long since by the Liberals in the religion of the West. Should we not be moving in this direction consciously and purposefully?

Cannot the Liberals again take up the observing, questioning, exploring tradition of the West, set it at the heart of their movement and hold steadfastly to it? Free of all dogma about having Truth already in hand by virtue of a divine revelation, can they not adopt once more and hold to the standards of the Western intellectual tradition *in religion*? Is anything so sacrosanct for the Liberals that it cannot be questioned or tested for its validity? In religion, as in life, faith has its place and it is important. But in religious fundamentals, can belief be substituted for the questioning, exploring tradition that lies at the heart of Western thought? Can belief any longer sustain us when we have developed an inquiring turn of mind? Can belief reach more surely into Reality than the observing, inquiring, exploring methods of Western thought? These are the questions today's Liberals must answer. They are the questions that are addressed in this book.

Notes

1. Thomas S. Kuhn, *The Structure of Scientific Revolutions,* 2d ed. (Chicago: University of Chicago Press, 1970), p. xi.

2. John Horgan, "Profile: Reluctant Revolutionary," *Scientific American* (May 1991): 40.

3. Hans Küng, *Christianity and the World Religions* (New York: Doubleday & Co., 1986), p. xvi.

4. Ibid.

5. *Webster's Ninth New Collegiate Dictionary* (Springfield, Mass: Merriam-Webster, Inc., 1985), p. 995.

6. Richard Feynman, "NOVA: The Pleasure of Finding Things Out" (Boston: WGBH Transcripts, PBS, 25 January 1983).

Part One

The Liberal Tradition
in the Religion of the West

The history of theology is the story of our human thinking about
God. The history of religion is the story of the way that thinking
has been reduced to official creeds, dogmas, and traditions. The history
of Liberalism in religion is the story of our human effort to break
through the official creeds, dogmas, and traditions in religion that
have congealed and become obstacles to the purposes they were
originally intended to serve. It is the story of the drive to be rid
of archaic modes of thought and practice and to press on into new
realms of understanding.

Liberalism in religion has often been identified with the scientific
method. It is all of that, but far wider in scope. In *The Western
Intellectual Tradition* J. Bronowski and Bruce Mazlish identified a
movement in human thought that centered in two ideas: (1) emphasis
upon the full development of the human personality, and (2) the
idea of freedom. Human fulfillment is unattainable without freedom,
they asserted. Our human need for freedom links the two ideas
together. They did not name the movement they identified "Liberalism," but no more concise statement of its essence is likely to
be made. The goal of the Western intellectual tradition is a balance
between power and dissent, they wrote. This is the heart of the movement. Dissent, questioning, and inquiry are creative in all fields. The
Western intellectual tradition is a tradition of questioning what is
traditional. Part One tells the story of its birth and growth in religion
in Western culture. That story is the story of Liberalism in the religion
of the West.

1

How It All Began

What is it that makes us human? Many different answers to that question have been given. Among them all, none is more generally agreed upon than this: the power of reflective thought distinguishes us. No other creature possesses it, at least none gives any indication of it that we can discern. We ourselves have acquired the capacity for reflective thought only very recently—probably some 30,000 or 40,000 years ago.

It was then, the scholars now surmise, that we humans first became aware of ourselves as persons. It was then that we began to reflect on our experiences, to piece them together into some kind of pattern and find meaning in them. Loren Eiseley tells the story in his inimitable prose-poetry. He writes: "The story of Eden is a greater allegory than we have ever guessed. For it was truly man who, walking memoryless through bars of sunlight and shade in the morning of the world, sat down and passed a wondering hand across his heavy forehead. Time and darkness, knowledge of good and evil, have walked with him ever since. . . . In the brief space between the beginning of the first ice age and that of the second . . . a new world of terror and loneliness appears to have been created in the soul of man. For the first time in four billion years a living creature had contemplated himself, and heard with a sudden unaccountable loneliness, the whisper of the wind in the night reeds. Perhaps he knew, there in the grass by the chill waters, that he had before him an immense journey."[1]

The Dawn of Religion

With the beginning of reflective thought there appeared one of the most basic aspects of human nature—religion. As we humans emerged from the haze of prehistory around ten thousand years ago, we were already endowed with elaborate theologies. The stories of the gods that crowd the pages of Homer are a case in point. So, too, with the stories in the Hebrew Bible, the Gilgamesh Epic and those that lie behind the Rig Veda. In prehistoric times it was the religions that answered humanity's questions at the deeper levels of consciousness. It was the priests and shamans, the prophets and seers who explained the meaning of life and who gave the people the assurance such answers bring. In myth and legend, song and story, they made it all clear, and fixed its meaning within the people by celebrating and reliving the events in their stories in awesome ceremonial, repeated on solemn occasions and in sacred places.

Myths, legends, and the rituals derived from them tend to settle into a pattern, however, as they are handed on from generation to generation. Over time they develop high resistance to change. Always the demand is present that the ancient stories be retold accurately and that the ceremonial by which they are reenacted not deviate from its familiar form. The words and ceremonies of an earlier time grow rigid. They then become sacred and finally unchangeable.

Nevertheless, surely from the beginning there were those with alert minds who had questions the priests and shamans and elders could not answer. Surely from the time we humans made our first forays into reflective thought there were those who responded to the answers from their elders with yet more questions. And surely from the beginning certain alert minds began to explain events, not through myths and legends and the intervention of gods and devils, but by natural causes. Someone struck by a falling tree, let us say, was seen as having been injured as the result of a high wind, not the whim of an angry god. A good catch of fish was seen to be the result of fishing where fish were plentiful, not the will of a friendly deity who brought the fish to the fisherman's net. These new and very different explanations of ordinary events introduced something new into religion that must have been very disruptive—the way of inquiry in place of the older assumption of constant divine intervention.

Thales of Miletus

How and when and where did so bold an idea originate? We do not know. Probably not among the priests and practitioners of religion. So far as our present historical records indicate, the idea of asking questions about the nature of our world originated in Ionia, a Greek colony on the eastern shore of the Mediterranean Sea in what today is called Asia Minor, in Turkey. We can date it to the early sixth century B.C.E. and place it in the city of Miletus and other neighboring communities.

Similar developments may well have occurred at other times and in other places; we do not know. The records that have come down to us from the ancient Greeks do, however, make it clear that a new way of thinking about basic things emerged in Ionia at the hands of obscure thinkers whose names were Thales, Anaximander, and Anaximines, all of Miletus, and also at the hands of Xenophanes in nearby Colophon.

If the records we have are accurate, Thales of Miletus was one of the boldest and most original thinkers the world has ever produced. Unfortunately, our information about him is very slight, but we can be reasonably certain about some of his activities. For example, he predicted an eclipse of the sun that occurred on May 28, 585 B.C.E. Predicting an eclipse of the sun so accurately as early as the sixth century B.C.E. tells us a great deal about him.

This single piece of information might lead us to say that Thales was an astronomer. Astronomy, however, which he probably learned from the Babylonians or Egyptians, was but one of his interests. Wise in the ways of government also, he advised the Ionians to set up a single deliberative chamber for the twelve city states of the area, and to place it, not in Miletus, his home town and the largest of the Ionian cities, but in Teos, because it was in the geographical center of the group. He is also reputed to have changed the course of the Halys River for military purposes, which might suggest that he was an engineer and a military strategist as well. He was also skilled in geometry, which means that he was a mathematician.

So far as our present records show, before Thales' time the human mind universally looked to narrative stories of gods and spirits, devils and hobgoblins in order to explain natural events. To the human mind at that time, much of what went on in the world resulted from the acts of the gods. Life was seen as a series of divine interventions in the affairs of earth, in effect as a continuing succession of miracles.

For Thales, apparently, such an explanation of things did not make sense, and he began speculating as to how the order of events might be explained better. He looked at the world of nature and asked himself what was going on there and why. If the whims of the gods did not explain it, he wondered, what would? Wrestling with these ideas, Thales hit on the idea that water ultimately is the explanation of all things. Few agreed with him, probably. His was too novel a way of attacking the problem. In fact, the idea that all things are essentially water must have seemed absurd to his contemporaries. Even Thales' great pupil, Anaximander, thinking for himself as Thales had done, rejected the water idea and concluded that things could be explained better by what he called "the Boundless."

The particular theories these early Greek thinkers developed are not important to us now. The Greeks themselves remembered these pioneers, not because their theories were right or wrong but because their way of thinking marked a fundamental departure from the age-old practice of explaining the nature of the world and the course of events by mythological tales. Anaximander, following Thales, derived his reputation not from his theory of the Boundless, but because he, like his mentor, also abandoned the way of myth and began speculating about the nature of the world based upon what he himself could see and understand.

It is easy to make too much of a figure like Thales, whom we can identify. Let us then take him as a symbol, rather than as an isolated genius. Let us take him as a symbol of the beginning of a basic revolution in human thinking, and soon after, at the hands of Xenophanes, a symbol of the beginning of a new mode of thinking in religion. The full significance and character of that kind of thinking *in religion* is gaining recognition only now in our own time.

The First Philosophers

Some scholars have argued that Anaximander had a greater and more original mind than Thales, because he made the first full-scale attempt

we know of to explain the nature of our world. He is the first cos-
mologist of whom we have any record. It seems to be agreed among
the authorities that he was the first to attempt a comprehensive
explanation of the multiple aspects of our world. He drew a map
of the little that was then known about the planet. He was even
said to have constructed a celestial globe and to have conducted
experiments of a primitive scientific nature.

We could go on. Anaximines, pupil and younger contemporary
of Anaximander, also of Miletus, is credited with having been the
first true scientist. He is said to have been the first to begin using
detailed observation to support his thinking even though we cannot
credit him with formulating and conducting experiments in the
technical sense of the term as we use it today. The two approaches,
that of Anaximander and that of Anaximines, taken together, have
been the way of science ever since. Scientists formulate hypotheses
by which to explain phenomena and then devise experiments by which
to validate the hypotheses.

I repeat, we could go on. But there is no need. These thinkers
in ancient Miletus, as a group, brought about a profound change
in human thinking. That should be enough to say. In fact their manner
of thinking was so new they seem not to have recognized the
significance of it themselves. They were aware that they were going
at things differently from their contemporaries. They saw that they
did not belong in any of the classes or groups their contemporaries
recognized. Puzzling over who they were and what they ought to
be called, Anaximander and Anaximines called themselves simply
Sophoi, meaning "the wise," not boastfully as we might think, but
because they were concerned with knowledge or wisdom. The name
"philosopher" by which the later Greeks came to know the early
Ionians was coined by Plato. The etymology of the word is clear.
It is a combination of *philō* (love) and *sophia* (wisdom) which means
that the philosopher is one who loves wisdom.

The concept, however, is basic, and it is one of which we shall
make continued use in these pages. With us today, as with the ancient
Greeks, philosophy means the love of wisdom—more specifically the
uninhibited, unrestricted pursuit of an understanding of reality,
including human values. The contrast we shall continually be drawing
here is between philosophy (the pursuit of wisdom or knowledge)

and religion (the worship of God or gods, and the belief that in religion we know by faith the Truth that religion alone possesses). Philosophy was born when the Ionians (or anyone else for that matter) ceased to rely on ancient religious lore, and sought wisdom and understanding through observation, reflection, and in open-ended inquiry into the nature of things.

Why Miletus?

Why did all this happen in Miletus? Why in Ionia? Why among the Greeks? Our records are too few and our perception of that time and place too dim to enable us to say with any certainty. What happened in Miletus might have happened anywhere in Greece, as the subsequent spread of Ionian modes of thought throughout Greece attests. It happened in Miletus, it is generally agreed, because of certain additional factors. In the seventh century B.C.E. Greece was a thriving young country emerging into civilization out of the recent barbarism of the past. As the mainland grew more crowded, colonies were established elsewhere in the Mediterranean basin, many of them along the west coast of Asia Minor, known as Ionia, across the Aegean Sea from the peninsula of the Peloponnesus.

Politically, Ionia was a loose federation of some twelve city states, and of these Miletus, at the mouth of the River Meander, was the largest, the most powerful and the most rapidly developing. Its material prosperity was notable. This in turn gave its citizens special opportunities for contact with other cultures, especially through the tradesmen and merchants who came there from distant lands. Miletus also enjoyed a strong cultural and literary tradition of its own dating back to the age of Homer. All these factors taken together seem to have provided the conditions within which a genius of the stature of Thales might appear, followed by others of similar ability and originality like Anaximander and Anaximines.

Walter Burkert in his recent history suggests that Ionian creativity in the field of natural philosophy and cosmology, in metaphysics, that is to say, was in no small part due to the character of Greek religion at that time. Greek religion had no documentary revelation; that is to say, it had no bible. Greek religion also had no founding figure in whom their religion centered: no Buddha, no Moses, no Christ. It had no organization of priests to develop, declare, teach and protect its ritual and doctrine. Greek religion had no monastic orders. Thus the inhibition toward independent thinking characteristic of Judaism and Christianity in ancient times was absent. Greek religion was characterized by ritual and myth, but neither was fixed, and the myths were not believed literally. They were celebrated and enjoyed by the people but did not amount to fixed dogma.

As we know, original thinking often results from the use of analogies. By the third millennium B.C.E., this had been the case with the Greek understanding of the origins of the Earth. They thought of the earth as having emerged from the sea and drying out. The idea was not original with them; they borrowed it from the Babylonians and the Egyptians. They, in turn, arrived at it by watching the Tigris, Euphrates, and Nile rivers recede each spring. They found that the river bottom, fertile from the winter's accumulation of silt, enabled them to grow crops to sustain them in the later dry season. The Greeks at that time assumed that the Earth was a flat disc, because that was how it looked to them. They thought of it as surrounded by a great river they called Okeanus. By analogy they conceived of the world as emerging from the River Okeanus and drying out as did the flood plains of the Nile, the Tigris, the Euphrates and other rivers when the spring freshets died down. Little wonder then that Thales, asking himself about the nature of things, guessed that water might be the ultimate explanation.

Thinking of that kind is characteristic of the human mind. Time for us is linear. Narrative, the relating of a succession of events, apparently is fundamental to our way of ordering experience. It was the genius of the Ionian natural philosophers to go about things differently. Seeking to understand and explain natural phenomena, they cut through the multitude of tales told by the poets and celebrated in religious rituals. They did not try to improve on the tales current in their day. Instead, they began looking at the world around them and tried to figure out what it all meant. Their answer was not new and better narratives, but new principles and concepts. They suggested that water was the basis of all things, or that fire was, or that earth, air, fire and water, all four were the basic principles by which the world could be understood and explained.

Also different about the ancient Greeks was the fact that none of them claimed to be God. No one of them claimed that his thinking came by divine revelation. Thus their teachings never became so sacrosanct they could not be inquired into, changed or simply discarded. That meant that growth, development, and correction were possible, whereas in the presence of deity, as in the case of Egypt, Israel, and other cultures, deification meant sanctity, and sanctity stifled imagination and experimentation. The early Greek philosophers had no documents of revelation with which to contend. No priesthood was watching to see that sacred traditions remained inviolate. No religious orders stood guard, devoting their lives to the protection and propagation of sacred writings, patterns of thought and sanctified rituals.

The Philosophers Move Into Religion

The thought of the Ionians was revolutionary in a dual sense. It marked a new way of going about the basic endeavor to understand and explain all of existence in its many dimensions. It also demolished the Greek theology of the time. Thales, Anaximander, and the other philosophers made no attack on the gods of Homer and Hesiod. They paid no attention to the gods of the Greek pantheon in particular at the outset. Either the philosophers saw no inconsistency between what they were saying and what the people believed about the Olympian deities, or, sensing the conflict, they chose to say nothing about it.

There was, however, one conspicuous exception, Xenophanes of Colophon. He, like Thales, did not think of himself as doing anything very new or extraordinary, at least as far as we know. Like Thales, he, too, was merely thinking about things and trying to make sense of it all. In doing so, however, he identified one of the most basic problems with which we humans have to deal: the conflict between the established teaching of the religions and the perceptions of inquiring minds.

Xenophanes, who had grown up in Miletus and had moved to Colophon, another of the Ionian cities, began speculating not about the nature of the natural world, but about the validity of the religious ideas and practices of the time. His was as revolutionary an idea as that of Thales had been a generation before, and was a part of the basic shift in thought then taking place. Xenophanes drew out the implications for Greek religion of the speculations of the Ionian natural philosophers. He sensed the inconsistency between the two thought structures and tried to resolve it.

Although only fragments of Xenophanes' writings have come down to us, we can see that, in attempting to build a consistent thought pattern out of the myths of Homer and the speculations of the Ionian philosophers, he took the very radical step of rejecting the thought pattern that was basic in his time, and of doing so openly. It was he who first said: "It is not the gods who make people, it is people who make gods." Recall the vivid and oft quoted fragment from one of his poems that has come down to us. Twenty-five hundred years ago Xenophanes wrote:

"Mortals consider that the gods are born, and that they have clothes and speech and bodies like their own.

"The Ethiopians say that their gods are snub-nosed and black, the Thracians that theirs have light blue eyes and red hair.

"But if cattle and horses or lions had hands or were able to draw with their hands and do the works that men can do, horses would draw the forms of the gods like horses, and cattle like cattle, and they would make their bodies such as they each had themselves."[2]

So far as our records show, Xenophanes was the first to realize and to say openly that humanity has had things backwards. Humanity, he said, creates God in its image, not the other way around. Talk about reinventing the wheel! How many people have made the same discovery for themselves! As I write (1993), a new book entitled *A History of God* is creating a small stir in literary and religious circles. Written by a former nun, it undertakes to show how the God of Judaism, of Christianity, and of Islam was created by the devotees of those religions, not the other way around as each of those religions taught from the beginning.

As a personal example, I well remember the Sunday I put before a somewhat startled Boston congregation the same idea, that God did not create man and woman in his image as Genesis states, but that it is we who create God out of our needs, our hopes and dreams. Since the dawn of human thought, I pointed out, men and women have created gods in their own image, or in the image of birds, snakes and turtles; mountains, the sun, the moon, and much more. I made my seemingly bold declaration unaware that Xenophanes of Colophon had said the same thing 2,500 years earlier. During three years of intensive study in a very liberal theological school I had learned the names of uncounted Old Testament figures, but do not recall ever having heard Xenophanes' name mentioned.

Blasphemy and Death in Athens

Among the few fragments and scraps of information about Xenophanes to be found in the ancient sources there is no intimation that he was ever called to account for his blasphemy against the gods of ancient Greece. Not so with those who came later, however, and who, like Xenophanes, were bold enough to express their thoughts openly. Conspicuous among these was a man named Anaxagoras. He was a brilliant thinker, a teacher and friend of Pericles, of Euripides, and probably of Socrates as well. Not surprisingly he, too, grew up in Ionia, where he doubtless was steeped in the tradition of independent speculation that still prevailed there. While still a young man he went to Athens, where he remained for the major part of his life.

Anaxagoras' teachings seem extraordinary to us even now. He saw the conflict between Ionian natural philosophy and the Homeric gods, and sought to resolve it by asserting that the gods of Homer were really only abstractions. The sun, to which all Athenians were accustomed to address prayers every morning and evening, was not a deity, he said. The sun is a mass of flaming matter of enormous size. He suggested further that both animals and humans originally sprang from warm, moist clay. The moon shines not by its own light, he said, but by the reflected light of the sun. He taught the atomic theory of matter, and was among the first to insist that change is real. Like Thales, he successfully predicted an eclipse of the sun, and to wide-eyed observers, demonstrated that air is not mere empty space but a compressible reality.

All this gave Pericles' enemies the opportunity for which they had been waiting. They first secured the passage of an antiblasphemy law, then, as an oblique attack on Pericles, brought his tutor and friend to trial for attacking the gods of the state. Anaxagoras was convicted, fined, and banished. He was saved from execution only by the intervention of Pericles himself—all of this in Athens, the cultural center of the Western world at that time.

Protagoras, a contemporary and fellow Athenian, was also exiled for blasphemy. Nothing of his work remains today except a single sentence from his essay entitled "On the Gods." Nevertheless, those few words undoubtedly summarize his basic viewpoint. He wrote, "Concerning the gods, I am unable to say whether they exist or not, nor, if they do, what they are like; there are many things which hinder us from knowledge; there is the obscurity of the subject and the shortness of human life."[3]

Today we have little trouble agreeing with Protagoras' doubts about the deities in the Greek pantheon. Like him we can find no reason for believing they ever existed, and like him we have no basis upon which to attempt any kind of description of them. We would also readily agree with him that many things hinder us from acquiring such knowledge, among them the obscurity of the subject matter and the fact that none of us has sufficient time to investigate so profound and complex a subject, owing to the shortness of our life span.

Seldom has anyone made a more profound observation. Who today would have any trouble agreeing with Protagoras' doubts about the deities in the Greek pantheon? Although most Greeks in ancient times doubtless accepted the pervasive thought structure of their culture, which included belief in the Homeric gods, no one today believes in them. Yet the world around, people still devoutly believe in the gods of their own culture as the Greeks believed in theirs. Yet are there not among such people today those who would say about their own gods what Protagoras said about his in his time and place? We miss the full impact of Protagoras' words unless we apply them to our own religion today. How many of us could or would say of the God we worship today what Protagoras said of the gods he was expected to worship some 2,400 years ago?

I repeat because the point cannot be overemphasized, we don't know who first began thinking as Thales, Xenophanes, and Protagoras did. There doubtless were many who came and went of whom the world has never heard. What we do know, and it is enough, is this:

somewhere, at some time the human mind began thinking this way. When that happened, religion in a new mode made its appearance on our planet. This new mode in religion, by fits and starts, has been growing among thoughtful people ever since. Today it is found worldwide. In the West uncounted millions have taken it as their chosen way. Most have done so unconsciously, vaguely, and uneasily, often completely unaware that they have, in their hearts and minds, departed from ancient and sacred religious modes of thought.

Are the people of the open mind and heart in religion atheists? The devout in all religions have usually said so. But they are mistaken—tragically so. To be sure, some dogmatic skeptics have declared that there is no God. But there is no evidence that Thales or Xenophanes or Protagoras made such a denial. Certainly I had no such thought and no such intent when I laid the god-making nature of humanity before my Boston congregation some forty years ago. The inquiring mind holds no dogma about the Deity. Open-minded inquiry is a way of resolving the conflict between those who do. Inquirers make no declaration of Truth about Deity. Rather, they invite one and all to a common pursuit of the question.

We have followed the story of the beginning of philosophy far enough. We have seen that the conflict between the way of philosophy and the way of traditional religion became explicit very early. All the world knows it soon brought to his death one of the great men of all time, Socrates of Athens. In the beginnings of philosophy, and in its application to religion, we are at the beginning of a new mode in religion. There we see a new paradigm for religion first beginning to take shape.

Notes

1. Loren Eiseley, *The Immense Journey* (New York: Vintage Books, Random House, 1946), p. 125.
2. G. S. Kirk and J. E. Raven, *The Pre-Socratic Philosophers* (New York: Cambridge University Press, 1971), p. 168.
3. F. M. Cornford, *Greek Religious Thought* (Boston: Beacon Press, 1950), p. 130.

2

The University Tradition

Philosophy rests upon a basic assumption about ourselves and our world. That assumption is opposite to and contradicts the basic assumption on which religion traditionally has rested. Philosophy assumes that to understand ourselves and our world we must go at the task of gathering knowledge in every conceivable way. Philosophy assumes further that we can succeed at this task, that by dint of human effort we can understand ourselves and our world, at least to a measurable degree.

Traditional religion, on the other hand, rests on the assumption that we can know final, ultimate Truth about the basics of life, but that our knowledge does not follow from human effort: the Truth we know in religion is a gift, given to us as a revelation from heaven, made available through seers, prophets, mystics and other specially endowed humans who are privileged to know eternal Truth and to transmit it to the rest of us.

The Intellectual Reawakening in Europe

Philosophy, the invention of the ancient Ionians, became a part of classical thought in the West, but it never became dominant. The idea of approaching knowledge with an open, inquiring mind never displaced the older religious concept of truth dispensed by the gods. The Greek spirit of inquiry, observation, experimentation and debate had already lost most of its momentum when Christianity became the official religion of the Roman Empire in the fourth century C.E.

33

From then on the body of doctrine held by the Church answered all basic questions. Its validity was established by the authority of the Church. Accordingly, dissent from official Church teachings was suppressed by force and cruelty. As a result independent thinking, questioning, experimenting, and debate virtually ceased.

This state of affairs continued for some five hundred years. Nevertheless, despite the mounting ruthlessness with which heresy was suppressed in the Roman Empire, independent thinking never quite died out. How much there may have been of it in actuality we have no way of knowing now. This much is clear to us: from the disintegration of the Roman Empire in the fifth century C.E. to the time we know as the Carolingian Renaissance in the ninth century, the light of learning and of critical, independent thinking burned very low in the West. Political, social, and economic chaos was the order of the day. Because of the turmoil people were concerned with simply staying alive more than anything else. As a result very little was accomplished in any field. In his *History of the Franks*, Gregory of Tours (538–593) gives a picture of the barbarization of the Church itself in a world of barbarism and violence. "The towns have let culture perish; learned men are not to be found. Woe to our times," he wrote.[1]

The story of the rebirth of learning in western Europe really begins with a man we ordinarily associate with war, conquest, and romantic poetry: Charles the Great, king of the Franks, known to history as Charlemagne. Under his leadership there occurred in western Europe, beginning in the ninth century, a movement we know today as the Carolingian Renaissance. It was an intellectual awakening that drew scholars from all over Europe.

The center of the revival was the Palace School that Charlemagne set up and which he himself attended. Those who gathered there were true scholars. They sought books wherever they could be found, laboriously making copies for themselves and others. They created original works of their own. They undertook to replace the often corrupt texts then in circulation with more accurate ones. The influence of the Palace School spread widely. As a result of it, libraries were established in monasteries where before there had been but few books. The libraries became centers for the production of more manuscripts, which in turn spread learning more widely throughout Europe.

Out of this movement the medieval universities arose. They made their appearance in response to a felt need. By the twelfth and thirteenth centuries a considerable body of learning had been accumulated, of which most people were only dimly aware, but about which there began to be a rising curiosity. As the news began to get around that a vast literature created by the Greeks and Romans, known only to a few scholars, lay hidden in Europe's libraries, the desire to get at it was kindled. The desire to read it, to acquire the knowledge the ancients had, mounted. In addition, by the time of the high Middle Ages, medieval "science" had developed a lore all its own. An expanding body of law was developing in both ecclesiastical and civil courts. Beyond these areas of learning there were the fields of medicine and mathematics, engineering, astronomy, and, of course, astrology, all of which required special training.

The universities were both the cause and the result of the re-awakening of the mood of inquiry. They prospered because of the thirst for learning that was felt throughout Europe at this time, stimulated by the awareness that there was much learning to be acquired. In the universities those with awareness taught those who lacked but wanted to acquire it. From this an unexpected result followed. Inquiring minds, gathered in one place, generated questions. The students not only stimulated one another and their teachers as well to new learning, they also gained support from one another in their questioning and in searching out answers that seemed more accurate and more adequate than those they already had. These answers in turn generated yet more questions from which still more and better answers came, and so on.

The corruption and lassitude that had eaten its way into the medieval Church also contributed to independent thought. The wealth, the high living, the immorality that characterized the Church generally in this period produced a mounting succession of protests, all from within the Church itself and in the name of its own ideals. In the Middle Ages the common people and most clerics had little understanding of the arguments by which Augustine had established the authority of the Church, but they had no difficulty whatever understanding the immorality and self-indulgence of the clergy. These practices were denounced, not only in terms of Catholic doctrine and Scripture but also in terms of common decency.

When the Church and the churchmen were challenged on the

basis of Scripture and by their own sense of what is fitting and proper, it was but a short step to the raising of doctrinal questions as well. When moral questions came and the questioning process was not denounced, intellectual questions soon followed. These questions meant inquiry, and when inquiry was reborn, the new paradigm for religion once again began taking shape in the West.

The Rediscovery of Human Fallibility in Religion

The medieval mind, steeped in dogmatic Christianity, thought of ideas as stable, fixed, and final. The great idea system developed by thinkers such as Augustine and, in particular, Thomas Aquinas in his *Summa Theologiae* had assumed that ideas remained stable in religion and in all other aspects of human thought as well. In the medieval universities, however, as thoughtful minds saw ideas changing, they could see themselves engaged in the process.

Peter Abelard's book *Yes and No* is a case in point. In that book, written probably about the year 1122, Abelard sets the writings of various Church fathers in juxtaposition with one another. His clear intent is to show what he himself had observed, that many of the ideas of the Church fathers had grown and changed over time and in some cases had ultimately come to contradict one another.

Alert medieval minds slowly became aware of something that was even more surprising. Knowledge, they discovered, was not always knowledge. Sometimes, they found, what had passed for knowledge for generations was actually false. Arnold of Brescia (1100?–1155), who had studied under Abelard, turned from a study of the writings of the Church fathers to a study of the Bible. For the twelfth century that was a radical step. Relying on the Bible text itself, he condemned the Church and churchmen alike for their worldliness and called for a return to the spiritual standards of the primitive church of apostolic times as it is set before us in the Holy Scriptures.

Lorenzo Valla (1406–1457) not only studied the Bible with close scrutiny, but went behind the text to speculate on its sources. He dared to ask heretofore unthinkable questions. For example: Did Moses himself actually write the Pentateuch? Tradition said he did, but Valla, basing his argument on the Bible itself, dared to say he could not have, a point on which all scholars agree today excepting, of course, the Fundamentalists.

Turning to Nature

As the Greeks had done a millennium earlier, scholars in the medieval universities began to think of the universe as something natural that could be comprehended by systematic investigation. Under the influence of the Church the medieval mind thought in terms of the supernatural, which the human mind should not even try to understand. In the twelfth century a few pioneering minds broke through that mental freeze and began a study of nature based upon observation, primitive (by our standards) experimentation, subsumed by the premise that the whole was logical, interconnected, and capable of being understood by the human mind. The evidence is to be found in the writings of Adelard of Bath in England, Thierry of Chartres, and William of Conches in France. All were students of Plato, of Aristotle's *Logic,* and of the writings of the Arabs (Averroes and Avicenna).

The change in the mode of thinking brought about by the development of the university system can be seen by turning to the dictionary. Consider the following list of words and the date of their first appearance in the English language (*Merriam Webster,* 9th edition).

1. Nature: fourteenth century. Derived from the Latin *natura.* The inherent character of a person or thing, also the external world in its entirety.

2. Natural: fourteenth century. Derived from the Latin *natura.*

3. Naturally: fourteenth century. Doing something according to natural character or ability.

4. Natural law: fourteenth century. A body of law derived from nature, and binding upon society in the absence of or in addition to positive law.

5. Natural science: fourteenth century. Any of the sciences (as physics, chemistry, or biology) that deal with matter, energy,

their interrelations and transformulations as they deal with objectively measurable phenomena.

6. Natural philosophy: fourteenth century. Derived from "natural science."

These changes accelerated in the period we call the Renaissance, as the following words and phrases coined at that time indicate:

1. Supernatural: 1526. Of or relating to an order of existence beyond the observable universe.

2. Natural history: 1567. A treatise on some aspect of nature.

3. Naturalist: 1587. A student of natural history.

4. Naturalism: 1641. A theory denying supernatural causes: scientific laws account for everything.

5. Natural theology: 1677. A theology deriving its knowledge of God from the study of nature independent of special revelation.

A New Institution in Human Society

Because independent thinking is a threat to any established order, be it that of the church or of the state, the inquiring mind might have been crushed again in the twelfth or thirteenth century had it not been institutionalized in a new social structure, the university. Started by churchmen within the Church, the medieval schools soon developed an identity of their own, and steadily moved outside the orbit of the Church. Today most but not all of our great universities, including those that began within the Church, are steadfastly and clearly independent of clerical control. Today the university ranks with government and religion among the most potent and pervasive of all social structures.

The importance of the university as an institution in human society cannot be exaggerated. The university system evolved out of the basic human need to know. It came into being out of our human yearning to understand ourselves and our world, and our desire to know what others have had to say on these questions. Universities came into being in medieval Europe because of the growing body of thought, ancient and contemporary, that medieval Europe was accumulating.

The university tradition reintroduced into Western thought a point of view that had taken form in ancient Greece but had hardly gained acceptance when it was replaced by the dogmatic, authoritarian approach to knowledge and understanding established by the Christian Church. This continued to be the attitude of the educated mind well into medieval times. In general the Middle Ages were concerned with outward conformity and the acceptance of authority more than with verifying the accuracy of statements or the sincerity of motive of the scholars. The open sexual immorality of the clergy, for example, posed no problem for the medieval Church but the advocacy of sexual freedom by a group called the "Free Spirits" was furiously hunted out and punished.

Thus, in the universities a new way of looking at the foundations of human thought emerged. Established as institutions of learning, they soon found themselves dealing with questions about the validity of the learning they were acquiring. In the medieval universities, not merely the gathering of knowledge was new. Also new was the idea that one should ask whether or not any purported item of knowledge was true, incomplete, or quite simply false. These were questions with which the ancient Greeks had struggled. Reborn in the medieval universities, they marked the rebirth of the inquiring mind in the West.

In the thousand years or more that have elapsed since the founding of the Palace School, the universities have become a dominant force in Western culture. Today, along with the church and the state, academe stands as one of the most powerful and influential of all our human institutions, with a distinctive role and character of its own. At its heart lies the demand, increasingly enforced with vigor and stringency, that what is taught shall be as valid, as accurate, and as true as the human mind can make it. The religion of the open mind and heart is the demand that the university tradition, in all the fierce allegiance to truth it has now attained, be introduced to and applied full scale, without stint to religion.

Note

1. Gordon Leff, *Medieval Thought* (Baltimore: Penguin Books, 1958), p. 57.

3

The Enlightenment

The pursuit of knowledge, the ideal of the university system, is one that few would challenge. Yet there lurks within it a very troublesome assumption. To seek knowledge means to inquire. It means asking questions. Asking questions means probing into the unknown. But we assume, and rightly so, that if the questioning process applies to the unknown it applies to the known as well. Asking questions, then, means probing what we suppose ourselves to know to see how sound our supposed knowledge may be.

The result can be very upsetting. Inquiry may lead to doubt. Doubt in turn leads to skepticism, and skepticism to denial and finally unbelief. In stark outline, that is what happened in Western culture during the Middle Ages and the Renaissance, culminating in the movement we know as the Enlightenment.

Pyrrhonism

Medieval times were marked by the dominance of traditional religious thinking. It was the way of authority. It meant accepting without question what was taught. Knowledge in basic matters was attained not by pursuing it, but by learning what had been revealed to the saints and sages of an earlier and more enlightened time.

We saw in the previous chapter how quickly and easily the knowledge the universities were gathering and disseminating came into question. At first the problem received little attention. The all-powerful authoritarian Church left no room for probing for error in what was supposed to be known already. In basic matters the Church declared the truth and few thought or dared to question it.

Questions soon emerged, nevertheless. Dissatisfied with the answers the Church offered, fueled by the ideas ancient authors had developed in the more open intellectual climate of classical times, a few writers began asking very mild questions. As an example, a problem arose with regard to documents from earlier times then being accumulated in the universities. They had come from a wide variety of sources: from Arab learning, which was far ahead of that in Western Europe at the time: and more directly from classical culture and the writings of the Greeks, the Romans, and other thinkers of ancient times.

As the body of documents grew in size questions began to arise with regard to specific items in it. For one thing, scholars found that copies of the same original manuscript did not always agree with one another. Some were obviously authentic, others quite obviously were not. Most could reasonably be questioned. How to tell the difference? How to assess the worth of each?

Implicit in the problem of the authenticity of aging documents, the provenance of which was unknown, lay the far more pervasive question, how can anyone be sure of anything? The question was not new. The Greeks had come upon it and wrestled with it a millennium before. In fact, in ancient times a school of thought had grown up out of that very troublesome idea. It was called Pyrrhonism, after its founder, Pyrrho of Elis, a philosopher of the fourth and third centuries B.C.E.

Pyrrho, influenced by Democritus and other philosophers before his time, became the first thorough-going skeptic of whom we have any record. He had studied abroad, and the impact of other cultures apparently had not been lost on him. In India and Persia he learned that many of the things that he as a Greek took for granted were not believed by the Indians and Persians. On the other hand, Pyrrho found himself quite unable to believe many of the things in which the Indians and Persians deeply believed. Beginning seriously to doubt what he himself had always supposed to be true, he slowly found himself driven to the position of ultimate skepticism. We cannot really know anything for sure, he concluded. We can only know that which we have tested to the uttermost and found to be true because its truth can be demonstrated. We cannot always be sure even of that, he said finally, because we can so easily fall into error.

René Descartes

Pyrrhonism enjoyed increasing attention in Western Europe during the Renaissance. In the Enlightenment it gained widespread popularity. The arguments of the Pyrrhonists greatly impressed René Descartes, the French mathematician of the seventeenth century, who became one of the great philosophers of that or of any time. Descartes also found himself asking how we could be sure of anything. In 1637 he gave his answer in a book entitled *Discourse on Method.* No one since has put the question more directly or answered it more satisfactorily. Descartes saw that if we are to answer the basic questions that both religion and philosophy attempt to answer, there are certain conditions we must meet. If we don't, our answers are worthless, however acceptable and/or desirable they may seem to be.

Our task, then, is to be rid of doubt. Seeking knowledge of which he could be really sure, Descartes began by trying to rid his mind of all the data lying there that he could not be sure of. He wound up with nothing certain but himself thinking about those problems. *Cogito ergo sum,* he concluded, casting it all in a single Latin aphorism meaning, "I think, therefore I am."

Try it yourself. Clear your mind of everything of which you cannot be absolutely certain. Can you get any further back than your own experience of yourself experiencing the experiences you have? Can you get to anything certain when you rely on what someone tells you? How can you be sure they really know what they think they know? When you reflect on your own experiences and try to make sense out of them, can you reach anything more certain?

Continuing, Descartes formulated in unforgettable language the problem of ever-besetting human error. In an opening paragraph of his *Discourse on Method,* he wrote: "I know how subject we are to delusion in whatever touches ourselves and also how much the judgments of our friends ought to be suspected when they are in our favor."[1] Following an autobiographical vein, Descartes relates how he had desired learning, but he then observes, "As soon as I had achieved the entire course of study at the close of which one is usually received into the ranks of the learned, I entirely changed my opinion. For I found myself embarrassed with so many doubts and errors that it seemed to me that the effort to instruct myself had no effect other than the increasing discovery of my own ignorance."

Finally, Descartes reports: "I came to the conclusion that there was no learning in the world such as I was formerly led to believe it to be." He then sums up his position in these words, "I always had an excessive desire to learn to distinguish the true from the false." He makes it clear that his purpose was not that of elaborating abstract philosophical principles. He wanted only to distinguish the true from the false "in order to see clearly in my actions and to walk with confidence in this life."

In these few paragraphs Descartes says it all. Error is our besetting human problem. If we want knowledge that is really knowledge—meaning knowledge, the validity of which we can depend upon—we have first to rid ourselves of error, at least insofar as we can. Otherwise we are twice deceived. We think we know, when we don't. In such a case we are not merely ignorant, we are misinformed. What we suppose ourselves to know and to be able to rely on is actually false, not reliable but unreliable. Yet unquestioningly we believe it to be true.

The greatness of Descartes lay in his insistence on the difference between truth and error, knowledge and opinion, certainty and theory. The ecclesiastical way of thinking had been central in medieval times. It meant accepting without question what one was taught. It was the way of attaining knowledge by faith. The modern way of thinking is opposite to that of the Middle Ages. It is, broadly speaking, the way of philosophy contrasted with the way of traditional religion. Philosophy is not the way of acceptance, it is the way of inquiry. It is not the way of Truth known by faith, it is the way of knowledge acquired by scrupulous attention to the fact of our human fallibility.

Descartes came at the end of the Middle Ages, when the culture of the West was in the process of grasping the importance of that distinction. He and other thinkers of his time mark the beginning of the period we call the Enlightenment. His thought and that of the Enlightenment he typifies also mark the beginning of modern times. What he succeeded in doing was to state as a principle what the universities had been slowly and painfully working through and thinking out since their founding some eight hundred years earlier. So slowly does human thought move; so slowly does an accepted pattern of thought achieve basic change. By Descartes's time the university tradition was working toward the standards of veracity and validity that characterize our universities today. He grasped the principle and stated it. He put into words what by that time was emerging as a basic principle of culture in the West, the problem of our human fallibility. With Descartes and with the Enlightenment the modern age was born.

David Hume

The true skeptic was, of course, the Scotsman David Hume; yet few people think of him that way. In our ordinary mental pigeonholes, the skeptic is an unpleasant doubter, a killjoy who questions everything. He makes everybody uncomfortable. The genial, urbane Hume did not fit the formula. He kept his skepticism as the theoretical outcome of his theoretical philosophy. Applying his skepticism to religion, he did so in a dialog in which he himself takes no position and in which the reader has to work hard to be clear as to what Hume, the author, is actually saying through his characters.

Unlike his counterpart and contemporary Voltaire, and many of the other leaders of the Enlightenment as well, Hume neither attacked nor satirized religion. Nevertheless, his philosophical skepticism which, by implication, clearly impugned traditional religion, apparently affected his career. His first work, *A Treatise of Human Nature,* in his own words "fell stillborn from the press." His contemporaries failed to see the significance we today find in his thinking. Still only in his thirties, he sought but was denied the Chair in Moral Philosophy at the University of Edinburgh. He then published a simplified version of his *Treatise* which he called *An Inquiry Concerning Human Understanding,* but that work, too, attracted little attention or praise.

When Hume was about forty years of age, he again sought and again failed to win a professorship at the University of Edinburgh. Beginning when he was about sixty, however, David Hume's peers at last saw the validity and the significance of his philosophy and he became a center of the intellectual and cultural life of Edinburgh until his death only a few years later.

Hume is important to us because of the resoluteness and clarity of mind with which he addressed the basic problem we humans come up against when we begin the questioning process. Where does it lead? Where does it stop? David Hume did not come out with an answer designed to please any person or group, as for example Bishop Berkeley had done when, shortly before, he affirmed that matter is not really real—one component of his effort to establish the existence of God. Hume reached a position of ultimate skepticism because that was where the sharpest, clearest reasoning of which he was capable took him.

Scholars disagree on the date when modern times began, but that need not trouble us. What is important is that Descartes as a pivotal figure, along with David Hume and countless others, marks the transition from the medieval to the modern way of thinking. Pivotal in that transition were the Enlightenment thinkers, many of whose works are still read and quoted today. Typical of them were Montaigne as well as Voltaire in France, John Locke in England, and Immanuel Kant in Germany.

The Enlightenment thinkers returned to the Greek mode of seeking truth, and were not reluctant to point out how it undermined the foundations of traditional religion. Negatively many of them went so far as to ridicule openly Christian claims to know absolute, final, incontrovertible truth. They took delight in exposing the inconsistencies and improbabilities that can be found in the Bible and in many Christian teachings.

On the positive side, the *philosophes*, as the French Enlightenment thinkers called themselves, sought to introduce into religion the standards of accuracy that had long since been accepted by scholars in the university tradition. They were moving toward what they called "Natural Religion." It was their name for a religion derived not from revelation or from ancient authorities but from observation, inquiry, reflection, and experimentation. Yet they made no attempt to found a new sect with new beliefs and practices. The Enlightenment was a movement that sought to bring together the teachings of the several existing religions and the body of knowledge being accumulated in other fields, all of it arrived at according to the highest standards of verifiability.

Observation, experimentation and critical thinking—these were the means by which the Enlightenment sought to expose and correct the errors and shortcomings to be found in traditional religious teachings. Their criticisms were not always constructive. Many of the philosophes were obviously angry. They were frustrated by the immobility of the clergy, infuriated by their often specious arguments, and revolted by the physical cruelty to which the churchmen so often resorted in their attempts to silence opposition to their views.

Overall, however, the work of the Enlightenment thinkers was positive in its purpose. They wanted to rescue religion from those whom they saw as its misguided supporters. By exposing and eliminating the errors and false arguments of the establishment they hoped to make religion more attractive. They wanted to develop a religion that would earn the respect of thoughtful men and women, in short to make religion consonant with the growing body of scientific thought in their time.

The philosophes believed above all else in hard-nosed thinking. Everything must be carefully examined, they held. Nothing was to be taken for granted, even the sacred teachings of Christianity. The Enlightenment was an age in which philosophy was dominant. It was an age that sought knowledge for the delight of discovery, and for the sheer pleasure of knowing, as well as for its usefulness. It was a movement that tried to draw all knowledge together, religion included, into a single consistent whole.

True Liberals today stand in the Enlightenment tradition not because they believe in Natural Religion, which most of them do, but because they believe we should be trying to do today what the natural religionists were trying to do in their time. Today's Liberals stand in the Enlightenment tradition not because they think we should try to build a theology based on contemporary science, which they do not, but because they want to close the gap between traditional theology and contemporary science.

Note

1. R. M. Eaton (ed.), *Descartes: Selections* (New York: Charles Scribner's Sons, 1927), p. 3.

4

The Liberal Vision Fades

Protestant Christianity flourished in the nineteenth century because
its leaders attempted boldly to meet the challenge of the Enlightenment. Not all of Protestantism, of course; numerically it remained
evangelical in mood and conservative in theology. But the leaders
in the churches and in the university theological schools, Harvard
and Chicago in particular, openly wrestled with the questions
thoughtful people were asking—questions inquiring minds had begun
asking in ancient Greece, that reemerged in the Renaissance, and were
clearly and forcefully put to the religious community by Enlightenment
thinkers. By the nineteenth century in the West, these questions were
openly discussed in the churches. Those who took the lead in doing
so were known as Liberals. They were the people who led in
advocating a more open or liberal approach to the issues that were
then coming to the fore, in particular as a result of the work of the
natural scientists.

Religious Liberalism

Religious Liberalism has been variously defined, but the consensus
seems to be that it is or was a movement in religion, prominent in
nineteenth-century Christianity, and became dominant in Protestantism in the late nineteenth and early twentieth centuries. It was an
attempt to bring together the thought pattern of Western culture and
that of traditional religion. *The Christian Century*, a middle of the
road Protestant weekly, looking back in 1934, summed it up very

well: "The difference between orthodoxy and liberalism was not a difference in doctrinal subject matter; it was (and is) a difference in the method of arriving at true beliefs. . . . That method is the method of inquiry, unencumbered by deference to certain static norms of truth"[1] A seemingly similar definition but with quite different emphasis, published in the *Century* in 1979, defined Liberalism much more narrowly as "comparatively receptive to the conclusions of the physical and human sciences."[2]

Both editorials missed the central point, however. Liberalism did indeed follow the method of inquiry, and it was increasingly receptive to science. But its differences with the main body of Christianity were differences of degree only. In the end the Liberals stood fast with Fundamentalists and Conservatives on a body of doctrine that had been established in Christianity in ancient times. This body of doctrine was not the result of inquiry. It was the result of the evolution of thought within the highly organized religions of the West, specifically Judaism, Christianity, and Islam. Its truth was known by faith. Protestant Liberals, with whom we shall be dealing primarily, tried to adopt the methods of inquiry advocated by Enlightenment thinkers and at the same time hold to the basic dogmas of the Christian faith.

These Liberals were clear about their own faith and they easily stated it. They believed in God the Father and in Christ the Son, Savior of all believers. They also believed in the Holy Spirit, an indwelling, guiding power, sustaining the faithful in all they said and did. They believed in the Bible as God's Word, his revelation to humanity. They believed in the forgiveness of sin, in redemption, in salvation, and in eternal life as the reward awaiting the faithful after death.

I do not write these words idly. I was one of them. As a young man, moving from youth to adulthood, in high school, college, and in graduate school, I was a Liberal Protestant Christian. It was not a position I had thought through and attained. Mine was an unexamined faith. My religious convictions simply reflected the outlook and practice of the Liberal Protestant Boston suburban Northern Baptist Church in which I had grown up. The faith of the church and its leaders was clear, and it never occurred to me to question it until, as my education progressed, I began to see inconsistencies between what I was learning in school and what I had been taught in the church.

Euphoria

To understand the Liberal movement in nineteenth-century Christianity, we who are living at the end of the twentieth century have first to sense something of the mounting euphoria of the decades preceding the outbreak of World War I. Looking back on the achievements of nineteenth-century science and technology; in the midst of the unbelievable accomplishments of the early twentieth—the airplane, the wireless, the telephone, phonograph, electric lights and electric power, the skyscraper, and the automobile—the people of that time were euphoric about the whole human enterprise, including the development of a new and much broader approach to religion.

The great Columbian Exposition in Chicago in 1892 and 1893 not only promised mechanical progress, the World's Parliament of Religions held in conjunction with it promised a new dawning in religious and political understanding. The First Peace Conference held at the Hague in August 1898 established the World Court. Little was accomplished at the outset, but the fact that the conference met at all and established the Court raised the hopes of peace-loving people everywhere. A Second Hague Peace Conference followed in 1906. Nothing concrete was accomplished at it, but hopes for peace were reenforced by the single fact that a second conference had met.

Protestant Liberalism in the nineteenth and twentieth centuries was one of the most prominent aspects of the euphoria of the time. In 1909 Charles William Eliot, president of Harvard University, published *The Religion of the Future*. In it he foresaw the eventual adoption of a religion according to Enlightenment principles, although he did not state his views that way. Believers in the broad principles of Liberalism do not usually think of themselves as belonging to any particular tradition or point of view. They think of themselves as following the highest standards of which they can conceive in their time and place. Eliot's book was typical of Liberal thinking at its zenith. It was nonsectarian, nondenominational, and factually non-Christian. Not anti-Christian, however; on that point we must be very clear. Early twentieth-century Protestant Liberals saw Liberal Christianity as the purest and best expression of religion we humans might expect to attain.

Neo-orthodoxy Takes Center Stage

Why did a movement that enjoyed such popularity in the highest circles of church, state, and academe suddenly disintegrate as Protestant Christian Liberalism did in the first part of the twentieth century? The answer to that question has to be stated both historically and theologically. The first blow was struck in the Roman Catholic Church under Pope Pius X. In the first decade of the twentieth century the Modernist movement in the Roman Church was running strong. It was essentially a demand for a revision of some of the ancient dogmas of the Church in the light of the findings of the scholars of the time. In 1907, Pius brought the movement to an abrupt end with his encyclical *Pascendi gregis* in which he condemned the Modernist movement and set up a system of censorship by which to demolish it.

In Protestantism the demise of Liberalism came about at the hands of its own leaders also. Their euphoria died in the disillusionment and the suffering of World War I and the initial collapse of their movement came at the hands of Karl Barth. He began his career as a German Lutheran pastor with the typical Liberal Protestant outlook of the time. As the war ground to a stalemate on the Western front, Barth found that his Liberal Protestant preaching meant little to his congregation. In an attempt to meet the spiritual needs of his people he began to shift to a more Bible-centered style of worship and preaching, and was heartened by the response of his congregation to the change.

From the Liberalism in which he had grown up Barth slowly moved toward a more evangelical approach. However we may now criticize his thought on philosophical or theological grounds, the most critical are forced to admit that Barth's evangelicalism in the real-life wartime situation he faced had a dimension of reality the older Liberalism could not match. For people numbed by the sheer horror of the slaughter the war involved, Liberalism, it seemed, had no message. New Testament evangelicalism did. Seeing this, Barth began preaching to his people about a God who is not only Lord of all, but also Father, Brother, and Friend. He rediscovered, he said, the God who reveals Himself in the Gospels, who Himself speaks directly to people and acts among and upon them.

In North America Protestant Liberalism did not reach its peak until the 1920s, the decade following World War I. Under the leadership of Harry Emerson Fosdick at the Riverside Church in New York; Shailer Matthews, Dean of the Divinity School at the University of Chicago; and countless others, Protestantism, it seemed, was moving toward an open adoption of Enlightenment principles.

But countercurrents were also flowing in Liberal circles in the 1920s. While Fundamentalism, because of its extreme theological, antirational position, was rejected by them, evangelicalism began gaining in strength. The younger ministers were reading Karl Barth. By the early 1930s, when the world was in a deep economic depression, and as the war clouds began to gather again in Europe, a young Lutheran minister named Reinhold Niebuhr, in an open and often unfair attack on Liberalism, began to summon the faithful back to the traditional dogmas of Christianity. The movement he virtually founded and certainly energized by the sheer force of his personality, his preaching and writing became known as "Neo-orthodoxy." It was exactly that—a new orthodoxy, a return to the central doctrines of traditional Christianity. In a few short years, during the early 1930s, Protestantism in the United States was completely overturned. Almost overnight, it seemed, the Liberal movement in Protestantism faded away and Neo-orthodoxy took its place. The liberal movement among the Jews, which had never been very strong, vanished in the Zionist movement and in the Holocaust of the Hitler years.

The spectacle of the great liberal teachers of the 1920s hastening back into the arms of orthodoxy during the 1930s has been reviewed often enough not to require another review here. The few Liberals who remained in the late 1930s had little to say. A small remnant, the Unitarians, Universalists, Ethical Culturists, a few Protestant mainliners, philosophers and others held to the older Liberalism. A small group of Humanists published the *Humanist Manifesto* in 1933. It was a clear forthright statement of Liberal principles and beliefs, but no movement of consequence grew out of it. By the time of World War II, Neo-orthodoxy had become firmly established as the dominant Protestant theological mode. Since that time, except for the rise of Christian evangelicalism, and TV hucksterism, no new movement has arisen to take its place.

Again, I do not speak idly. As a student in a "Liberal" theological school, I watched these developments in amazement. Not that Karl Barth, Reinhold Niebuhr and the rest were wrong about the shallowness of the Liberalism of those days: they were right. My incredulity lay in the fact that Neo-orthodoxy swept all before it while leaving unanswered the questions that had brought into existence the Liberalism its leaders had so recently given up. Biblical criticism had shown how very human a document the Bible is. Modern science had shown how farfetched and simplistic was the Bible's geology and psychology, its anthropology, history, and metaphysics. Liberal Protestantism had undertaken to resolve these inconsistencies and contradictions. They had been multiplying during the eighteenth, nineteenth, twentieth centuries, and earlier. The Liberal goal was to reconcile the "truths" traditional religion claimed to hold, with the demonstrable knowledge and understanding the Western mind had been accumulating. Specifically, the Liberals sought answers to the questions the Enlightenment thinkers had asked. But they had not found the answers they sought. The issues philosophers raised had not been resolved, they had been bypassed. How, I wondered, could it all be explained?

Why Liberalism Collapsed

Many reasons for the collapse of Liberalism have been given, most of them cosmological or metaphysical in character. Its doctrine of God was not powerful enough (Karl Barth). Its doctrine of Man was not realistic enough (Reinhold Niebuhr). My own view, at the time— one that was widely held—was that Liberalism was empty at the core. At its heart lay abstractions people did not grasp and principles that lacked persuasive power. Seeking intellectual respectability, Liberalism lost the central ingredients of all religion—the ability to stir people, to inspire them, and to provide them with a philosophy of life by which they might confidently live.

Over a century ago Otto Pfleiderer, a German philosopher, wrote: "Spinoza set the problem for the philosophy of religion. It is still the same today. Why is popular religion irrational but effective? Why is the religion of the philosophers rational but ineffective?"[3] In fact, the problem, like all the others with which the inquiring mind deals, goes back to ancient times. George Santayana, commenting on the philosophy of Plotinus, a Roman thinker of the third century C.E., asked himself why the completely rational religion that Plotinus constructed never caught on.

Answering his own question, Santayana wrote: "The bread of Plotinus was a stone, the heart cannot feed on thin and elaborate abstractions. . . . People will often accept the baldest fictions as truth; but it is impossible for them to give meaning to cautious conceptions or to grow to love categories of logic. . . . Religion must spring from the people; it must draw its form from tradition and its substance from the natural imagination and conscience. The Neo-Platonism (of Plotinus) drew both form and substance from a system of abstract thought."[4] As with Neo-Platonism so, too, with twentieth-century Protestant Liberalism; in its attempt to make room for the God of the galaxies it lost the God of Karl Barth and the New Testament, to whom it also clung.

Important as this factor was—and I would not minimize it— the weakness of Liberal theology was the symptom, not the cause of the problem. No one seemed to sense what it was. Certainly I did not, nor did my teachers or colleagues. The real reason for the collapse of Liberalism was a fatal flaw at its heart, that of a basic self-contradiction in its position and purpose.

Liberalism tried to keep intact the thought structure it had inherited from a Christianity the central dogmas of which it was at the same time undermining. It was trying to bring into religion modern scientific discoveries and modern patterns of thought while holding to ancient Christian dogmas. It was trying to think according to the world view of the ancients and that of the modern West, both at the same time.

The Liberals had seen clearly the errors and shortcomings of the older orthodoxy. As a remedy, they had chosen the way of modification and patchwork. To do so seemed logical enough. They had been brought up to accept the truths of modern scientific discovery and at the same time the revealed truths of the Christian tradition. To try to make the new discoveries of the modern age a part of their ancient faith was the natural course for them to have taken. The result, however, was an assembly of separate insights, each worthy taken by itself perhaps, but too often inconsistent and contradictory when the several parts were put together.

Krister Stendahl, former Dean and Chaplain of the Divinity School at Harvard University, once remarked in an informal gathering, "Liberalism is the view that religious thought and institutions should be freed from the restraints of tradition." The actions and the writings of the Liberals testify to the accuracy of his observation. But Liberals seem not to have realized that at the root of the tradition from which they sought release lay a doctrine that denied their right to do it.

A contemporary Liberal Christian feminist writes in eloquent support of this point: "Nobody loves a liberal theologian: she or he is neither fish, flesh, nor fowl—juggling metaphysical categories culled from secular philosophies with biblical and traditional concepts from his or her religious heritage, trying to satisfy two audiences whose demands and needs are usually very unalike if not flatly opposed. . . . Few love liberal Christians. They are neither properly religious nor properly philosophical."

A contemporary Bible scholar makes the same point with regard to Neo-orthodoxy. The Neo-orthodox compromise, he writes: "that of accepting both the validity of historical criticism and the truth-guarantee of revelation is inherently self-contradictory. . . . The Biblical Theology Movement, which attempted to do this, died of its own contradictions in the late 1960s."

There was much talk of irony in the latter-day attack on Liberalism. The true irony in the movement lay in its falling into the very error it sought to correct. The Liberals saw the need to update ancient doctrine. While doing so they quite logically tried to keep intact the foundations on which that doctrine rested, but the principle on which they were doing their updating required hard factual scrutiny of those very doctrines. When the Liberals refused to take that last step, when they declared the basic Christian dogmas inviolate, they left a flaw at the heart of their movement that ultimately destroyed it.

The Liberals had been moving toward a new concept of what religion is, apparently unaware that they were doing so. They had in fact embraced a large part of that concept. Their basic mindset was that of Western culture, and it was slowly becoming a part of their religion. They had consciously and openly given up many of the religious ideas in which they had been reared. But called upon consciously to give up the most basic articles of their religious faith, they found themselves unwilling to do so. In the end Liberalism collapsed, destroyed by its own inner contradictions.

Some of the questions raised by the Enlightenment, emergent in Liberalism and bypassed by Neo-orthodoxy, were reconsidered in the movements of the 1960s known as Christian Secularism and the Death of God. But these movements soon faded. Today those questions no longer interest most theologians and many say so openly. Yet there they remain, still unanswered, draining off the strength and vitality of the established religions as we move toward the twenty-first century.

The End of the War Between Science and Religion

In the nineteenth century a few writers on the side of the Liberals as well as on the side of the Fundamentalists and Evangelicals saw the scope of the problem clearly. They spoke openly of the "war" between science and religion that resulted from it. In 1874, J. W. Draper, a professor of history in the University of New York, published a book entitled *A History of the Conflict Between Religion and Science.* He concluded by finding a "great impending intellectual crisis which Christendom must soon inevitably witness. . . . The time approaches," he said, "when men must take their choice between quiescent immobile faith and ever-advancing Science."[5]

Twenty years later, in 1896, Andrew D. White, president and professor of history at Cornell University published a two-volume study entitled *A History of the Warfare of Science with Theology in Christendom.* In it he expounded at length on the conflict Draper had outlined, bolstering his arguments with fresh data that science had been accumulating during the intervening years. Tracing the conflict between religion and science, he did not hesitate to label it a "war." White concluded his impressive study by predicting the triumph of enlightened reason in all things religious. "Modern science . . . has acted powerfully," he wrote, "to dissolve away the theories and dogmas of the older theological interpretation [and] has been active in a reconstruction and recrystallization of truth; and very powerful in this reconstruction have been the evolution doctrines which have grown out of the thought and work of men like Darwin and Herbert Spencer."[6]

With the demise of Liberal Protestantism in the 1930s, it was taken for granted that religion had won the "war," or that at least, contrary to the predictions of Draper, White, and others, traditional religion had not been vanquished. A popular solution of the problem today runs: religion has its sphere, which science is not competent to enter, while the sphere of science is one that religion is not competent to enter.

Protestant Liberals failed to see that the story of religion in the culture of the West is the story of the emergence of a new paradigm for religion and that they had played a central part in it. The story tells how religious thought in the West has, slowly, silently, almost unnoticably, become consonant with the Western intellectual tradition. The result is a new concept of what religion is—in short, a new paradigm for religion. The new paradigm requires a mind that is open to new knowledge and understanding and a heart that is open to people of all varieties of faith. In the new paradigm for religion Hans Küng's appraisal of the religious situation worldwide is seen as accurate. The world is, as he says, moving toward de facto ecumenism, the mutual acceptance on the part of each of us of religions other than our own.

When you come right down to it there are only two kinds of religion. In the multitude of differences in thought and practice among them all, each in the end is either open or closed. Each is either exclusive or inclusive in character. Each either claims special status for itself through a special revelation or strives to show how all of the teachings of all the religions point humanity to a common ideal to which each makes its special contribution. The first type pits the religions against one another in a contest for supremacy; the second does not. Instead, it builds bridges between the several religions. The second type would link arms, join hands and finally minds and hearts among all the people of all the religions. That is the essence of the new paradigm for religion.

A few lines from Edwin Markham, slightly revised, sum it up:

> They drew a circle that shut us out
> Heretics, Rebels, people to flout.
> But we had the love and the wit to win:
> We drew a circle that took them in.[7]

Notes

1. "Is Liberalism Bankrupt?" *Christian Century* (July 4–11, 1984): 664.

2. Harvey Seifert, "Unrecognized Internal Threats to Liberal Churches," *Christian Century* (October 31, 1979): 1057.

3. Otto Pfleiderer, *Philosophy of Religion*, vol. 1 (London: Williams and Norgate, 1886), p. 67.

4. George Santayana, *Interpretations of Poetry and Religion* (New York: Charles Scribner's Sons, 1900), p. 80.

5. J. W. Draper, *A History of the Conflict Between Religion and Science* (New York: D. Appleton & Co., 1875), p. 364.

6. Andrew D. White, *A History of the Warfare of Science with Theology in Christendom*, vol. 2 (New York: D. Appleton & Co., 1896), p. 394.

7. Edwin Markham, *The Shoes of Happiness and Other Poems* (New York: Doubleday, Page & Co., 1915), p. 1.

Part Two

Belief

"I have no trouble with the critical way in religion," a good friend and colleague once remarked. "I am for it, all the way. But when you are all through criticizing traditional beliefs, what do you put in their place? What do *you* believe? What do *you* live by?"

Otto Pfleiderer and George Santayana, Karl Barth and Reinhold Niebuhr were right. It is all well and good for the Liberals to try to bring religion into line with the standards of "secular" thought in the West. But when you abandon the thought structure Christianity has built over two thousand years, by which uncounted millions of people have lived and are still living their lives, what do you offer them that is more persuasive and makes for better living?

Liberalism stands or falls on its ability to answer this question, yet the Liberals give it all too little attention. The reason is that a series of questions pressed all the way back to the most basic questions you can ask yields a surprise. Such an inquiry does not yield answers, at least not at the outset. Inquiry pressed as far as it will go produces a set of standards any answers you find must meet if they are to be persuasive to the contemporary mind.

What are some of these standards? Can the process of inquiry never yield a thought pattern, a theology, a philosophy by which we may live our lives? Let us see.

5

Testing

The position of the Liberal Protestants was essentially that of the Enlightenment. They never said so, but the case is clear. They felt the Western intellectual tradition had raised serious questions for religion that must be dealt with. Back of them all lay the root question: how can we be sure of the truth of our beliefs? We humans are making mistakes and deceiving one another all the time. In religion how do we surmount our human fallibility? Can we? What enables us to do it?

The Western intellectual tradition has an answer to that question. We can surmount our fallibility and we do it by testing. We test the validity of every assertion anyone makes with every device we can think of. If we would know whether a statement is true or false we check it out by every means we can devise. However, on this point the mindset of the West and the mindset of Western religion divide. The religions hold that in their area, Truth is not arrived at by checking and testing. Truth is already in hand before the questioning process starts. Truth in religion comes by revelation. It is established by the authority of the church. If God has chosen to reveal Truth to humanity, it need not be tested. It is to be accepted and held by faith. In the Western intellectual tradition, however, any supposed truth, be it religious or of any other kind, is tested for validity in every conceivable way before it is accepted. Even then its final truth is seen as tentative only.

We begin then with a belief in the importance, and in the fruitfulness of testing. But is there really anything novel in that? Do not we all examine our beliefs constantly, inquirer and conservative alike? Yes, but only to a certain point. For nearly all religious people there comes a point when the questioning stops and the testing is concluded. Then faith steps in, and believing begins, resting upon the authority of the religion we hold as ours. By contrast, in the Western intellectual tradition the questioning stops only when there are no more questions to ask. Testing is given up only when no new tests can be devised.

Our Human Fallibility

That was the driving force of the Enlightenment. The philosophes felt the need to deal with the fact of human error. Inquiry has no point unless inquirers can be assured that the answers to whatever questions are being asked are as valid, accurate, and complete as possible. For the inquirer all errors must be identified and corrected. Deceit must be searched out and eliminated, self-deceit as well as intentional misrepresentation.

The ancient Greeks were clear that we humans are fallible. Parmenides, in the sixth century B.C.E., concluded, after thinking the problem all the way through, that we cannot rely on our senses; that we cannot be certain it is truth that they are conveying to us. Fallibility is a major aspect of us humans. We make mistakes all the time, errors of judgment and observation. We deceive others, some intentionally and others unintentionally. We make mistakes, even when we go to the greatest lengths to avoid them. We are error prone, all of us. Overcoming this limitation is a lifelong concern for every one of us. We humans are so liable to make mistakes, in fact, that we err even when we know we are likely to do so and have taken every possible precaution against it.

Anyone who has tried to count the money taken in at a church fair or garage sale or public event knows how astonishingly difficult it is to total the bills and change and come out with the same result that other counters reach. In guarding against error, we are faced with the further problem of willful deception on the part of others. It is a difficulty from which, unhappily, we are never free.

Human history offers all too many instances of beliefs once stoutly adhered to, but subsequently proved erroneous. The world is not flat as it was once universally assumed to be; the sun does not go around it; the will of the gods does not explain either the weather or human misfortune. Personal sacrifice, including that most appalling of all offerings, human sacrifice, is no longer thought to have accomplished anything but the agony it brought to those who participated in it.

Error and Villainy in Computers

The problems that worried Descartes and Hume seem elementary today. They are. Error and deceit continue to plague us but we grow increasingly intolerant of them. The computer has made us peculiarly alert to both. In a computer small errors can build into gigantic problems because they are so easily made and often so difficult to ferret out and eliminate. The damage that can be done by intentionally destructive programming is now only beginning to be understood and guarded against. As the computer becomes ubiquitous, new vistas of as yet unimagined proportions open up for the ancient problems of human error, mischief, and downright evil. Ways to invade private computer linkages have been devised. Taking an analogy from biology, we talk about computer "viruses," programs that can foul up or even erase altogether data of unique value.

In March 1992 an ingeniously designed virus capable of hiding, replicating itself, and at a given time emerging to erase important data in computer software around the world was launched in the computer world. Will it be a permanent problem with computer technology? Who can say? What we can say with assurance is that the computer virus warns the most optimistic among us that human error is not a thing of the past, that our fallibility persists into this, the age of science, and that we have as great a need to guard against calculated villainy as we have ever had.

The problem is not new, only the technology. But the human creature who is responsible for both remains with her/his potential for error, deceit, and evil with dire consequences for us all. In the light of these awesome possibilities we must reexamine the religions' claims to hold knowledge that transcends our human limitations. Would that the religions could achieve so much. Would that there existed an area of human interest and endeavor where we humans were error-free and unable to be deceived.

Sacred Documents

Almost every religion has its sacred literature. The religions of the world offer so many holy books it would be impossible to list all of them. Over one hundred years ago (1875) Max Müller published *The Sacred Books of the East*. There were fifty-one volumes in the set. As we might expect, each religion regards its own sacred literature as valid, true, and right. Difficult passages are explained away. Unlikely stories are interpreted and belief in them is invited on the ground that when their deeper meaning has been seen and understood, then belief is possible.

In stating its beliefs traditional religion begins in the past. Its starting point is ancient documents regarded as sacred, or traditions, practices, and structures regarded as sacred because of their supposedly divine origin. But if we begin with ancient documents, they immediately raise questions. Are they genuine? Some, the Bible for instance, the Book of Mormon for another, claim to have been written by God's own hand. But does that prove they were? Could not the authors have been mistaken? Many ancient documents, claiming divine origin for themselves, following a careful review, have been rejected as spurious by subsequent generations. In Christianity, for example, the Apocrypha, the pseudepigrapha, and the Gnostic Gospels as well were all at one time held by one group or another to have been divine in origin, but are not now.

Examples abound of the revision in our thinking that today's scholarship invites when we turn to the Bible. In October 1988, the news media headlined a story: "Lord's Prayer Isn't His, Panel of Scholars Say." But it was not news at all to students familiar with biblical criticism. Generations of observant scholars had long since shown that the prayer of Jesus in the Sermon on the Mount[1] was obviously an assembly of time-worn, well-polished petitions, not a spontaneous utterance. What made the media story newsworthy after some two hundred years, during which the churchmen scoffed at such an idea and denounced it, was that a panel of highly respected

Roman Catholic and Protestant scholars working together had formally adopted this position and had done so by a nearly unanimous vote.

History records many an instance of well intentioned yet deliberate misrepresentation by high-ranking ecclesiastics, and the practice has continued intermittently into our own time. As an example, "medieval" Catholic marriage manuals circulating in the Roman Church between 1930 and 1965 have since been shown not to have been written in the Middle Ages but in the same years—between 1930 and 1965—in which they made their appearance. Their purpose was noble, at least in the minds of the authors, namely to support the traditional Roman Catholic concept of womanhood. Nevertheless, noble in motive or not, they were a calculated deception made by high-ranking churchmen.

A 1985 study of biblical theology undertaken by traditionalist scholars shows that many a current Bible dictionary endeavors to present archeological data as supporting the Bible when the opposite is clearly the case.[2] To bolster conservative religious views, they use outdated entries from older archeological sources. Often they abandon the factual approach one looks for in dictionaries and embrace polemics designed to show that the Bible is literally true. In some cases they go so far as to reprint data from older writings long since discredited.

In the mass of books now resting on the shelves of the world's libraries there is wisdom and inspiration of which religious people can be proud and of which they should make use. However, on those same shelves also rest far too much error and folly. In the West in virtually all disciplines we seek out the errors and deceits that descend to us from an earlier time in all the disciplines but religion. There, too often, we cling to what has come down to us from ancient times seemingly fearful to modify it or give it up, lest, by eliminating the errors we find in it, we lose the goodness that makes it precious to us. In the new paradigm for religion, this attitude is seen as a grave mistake. As the Western intellectual tradition calls upon us to seek out the errors and deceptions of the past and eliminate them in so-called secular fields, so does the open mind and heart demand that we do so in religion.

Criticism in Traditional Religion

The idea of testing the validity of one's religion is not new, of course. In a very real sense it has always been present. The human mind by nature learns very early to check things for deception and error. We are always trying to detect and eliminate error and deceit from what we suppose ourselves to know. The shaman, whose task it was to foretell the seasons, corrected his forecasting as he learned the regularities of motion in the sun, the moon and the stars. The scribe in his scriptorium learned to correct clerical errors he detected in ancient manuscripts. The priest, celebrating temple rituals, learned which of them were the most meaningful to the worshipper and revised his practices accordingly. Civilization and culture are, among other things, an elaborate structure through which we get things straightened out. Both assist us in distinguishing truth from falsehood, accuracy from error, half-truths from whole truths, and adequate statements from those that are inadequate.

Traditional religionists believe themselves to be no less aware of our human tendency to err than Enlightenment thinkers, and no less conscientious in guarding against it. For example, they examine and test the evidence for alleged miracles in every possible way. But there is a difference and it lies in the rigor with which these standards are applied in the two traditions. We recall that Augustine was a sharp clear-minded critic of religious ideas. But we also recall there was a whole body of Christian thought into which he did not inquire and on the validity of which he offered no opinion of any kind. These things, he told the believers, were to be taken on faith. In the new paradigm for religion no such demand is heard. There the call is for testing, applied all the way to the end of the thinking, fact-finding process.

No Infallibility

In making flat, clear statements of their position, critical thinkers find themselves in an all-too-familiar place. They seem to be denying one of the most cherished of the dogmas of traditional religion. To assert flatly that we humans are fallible is for example to deny by implication the ancient and central doctrine of infallibility in the area of religion. It is to assert, seemingly dogmatically, that religion cannot know with certainty what we readily admit we do not know in virtually all other areas of human activity.

In the eyes of critically minded people the idea of infallibility does not solve, but only compounds the problem of human error. The idea rests on the doctrine of revelation. But that doctrine is also unsupported and you cannot reinforce one unsupported statement with another. Religion cannot be made an exception to any general rule, the critical mind would argue. Religion and life are one.

The idea of infallibility in religion cannot be proved right or wrong. We can, however, say without hesitation that experience teaches us to be wary when anyone makes such a claim. We can all too readily demonstrate our human fallibility. And we cannot make ourselves infallible by declaring that we are as, for example, the Vatican Council of 1870 attempted to do.

The First Requirement

The first belief we discern in the religion of the open mind and heart turns out not to be an article of cosmic faith but a standard any belief we hold must meet. If we are to delineate Reality—and that is what we expect of religion—our delineations, however attractive, must be able to withstand harsh and detailed scrutiny. If our religion offers us a belief in miracles or in the afterlife, the forgiveness of sins, or the promise of divine guidance, these beliefs will have to remain intact after we have probed into them with the most far-reaching questions we can devise. Any belief that cannot stand up under such an examination will be of little use to us. A belief half believed is not a conviction, it is a dogma. It cannot sustain us in life's crises when we need our religion most.

In the new paradigm for religion, then, a statement of belief begins not with a cosmic declaration like belief in God, but with a statement of fact. *We humans are fallible creatures.* Our fallibility is not a matter of belief, it is an all too evident reality. The sun rises and sets, the seasons follow one another in succession. The tides rise and fall. Joy and sorrow, victory and defeat are aspects of the human condition.

So, too, is our fallibility a permanent, incontrovertible aspect of our makeup. We humans, all of us, are imperfect, incomplete people, far from totally competent. We are plainly and simply error-prone, and not above deceiving one another for purposes both good and evil.

The purpose of believing in religion is to provide us with a thought pattern by which to understand what it means to be alive, and so to know how to live. We need to know how to deal with the multiple important choices life continually lays before us. A thoroughly tested thought structure, in which we deeply believe because it has been thoroughly tested, gives us the confidence we need. We cannot live our lives by a creed laced with doubt as to its validity. Intolerable in any aspect of life, falsity must be completely lacking in religion, or religion itself is destroyed. Aimed at the highest and best we can conceive, religion cannot stand with falsehood. Whichever prevails destroys the other. To insist upon, to implement and always to exercise this principle is the reason for the birth and growth of the Western intellectual tradition. Richard Feynman once observed, "The key to science is a 'kind of scientific integrity,' a principle of scientific thought that corresponds to a kind of utter honesty—a kind of leaning over backwards. For example, if you're doing an experiment, you should report everything that you think might make it invalid—not only what you think is right about it."[3]

Testing is not done by the timid. It is the way of those who are fearless and bold. Testing is not the choice of those who fear to be wrong. It is the way of those who are determined to overcome error and shortsightedness if they can. "Accuracy is a duty, not a virtue," A. E. Housman once observed. In the Western intellectual tradition it is a goal to be striven for, whatever the cost.

Notes

1. Matthew 6:9–13 and Luke 11:2–4.

2. James C. Moyer and Victor H. Matthews, "The Use and Abuse of Archeology in Current One-Volume Bible Dictionaries," *Biblical Archeologist* (December 1985): 222.

3. Richard Feynman, "NOVA: The Pleasure of Finding Things Out" (Boston: WGBH Transcripts, PBS, 25 January 1983), p. 10.

6

Questing

If our human capacity for error is a severe limitation, some of our other most basic characteristics, namely our probing curiosity, our passion to understand, our imagination, and our ability to conceptualize are among our greatest assets. As we constantly test and check the adequacy and validity of what we suppose ourselves to know, so also do we constantly seek a better understanding of what we already know, and we seek yet more to penetrate into that which is not yet known. We are forever trying to clarify and really to comprehend that which we barely perceive and are only beginning to understand.

What Questing Means

As testing means checking everything we suppose ourselves to know and understand, questing means moving out into realms where we are uncomprehending and ignorant. Questing means pushing beyond the known into the unknown. It means trying to penetrate through the concepts we have already formulated to new ones we only dimly perceive. Older than human history, the practice of seeking new understanding, once largely unconscious, has been growing quietly through the centuries until it is now worldwide as a conscious endeavor, although far from having attained universal acceptance as yet.

Questing, adventure, imagination—all these bespeak our human urge to probe into ignorance until it becomes comprehension and knowledge. Questing is the most essential ingredient in the new paradigm for religion. It rises within us of its own accord. The impulse

71

lurks in nearly all of us, waiting to lay a compelling hand upon us, ever ready to draw us out beyond the world which we know at first hand into the world that might be, a world not as yet known, a world the nature of which is still to be grasped.

Questing means pushing beyond concepts we already have to new ones we are in the process of formulating, as when Niels Bohr and a small group of atomic physicists in Copenhagen and Goettingen back in 1922 conceived quantum mechanics. It means creating something essentially new as against merely improving the old. Alfred North Whitehead called this process "the adventure of ideas." It was the title he chose for the third book in his great trilogy which began with the publication of *Science and the Modern World* in 1925. "Adventure is essential," he wrote. "It is the search for new perfections."[1] On another occasion he remarked that, "Human life is driven forward by its dim apprehension of notions too general for existing language."[2] The truth in this observation is demonstrated by the result that follows upon such dim apprehensions when at last they are understood and made clear. Concepts which today can easily be taught to the young only yesterday eluded the grasp of the greatest intellects, Herbert Butterfield observed.

The historian Daniel Boorstin wrote, "The most promising words ever written on the map of human knowledge are *terra incognita*—unknown territory." But there are obstacles to discovery, he continued. These are the illusions of knowledge which later we discover to have been error. "Only against the forgotten backdrop of the received common sense and myths of their time can we begin to sense the courage, the rashness, the heroic imaginative thrusts of the great discoverers. They had to battle against the current 'facts' and dogmas of the learned."[3] It is with these obstacles, the immobility of basic theological ideas in traditional religion with which the inquiring mind is most concerned.

New Ideas

Even basic innovations are never wholly new, of course. Everybody's favorite example of thinking up a "new" idea that is in fact very old is that of the wheel. No need to reinvent it, we say. But the wheel, like most of the fundamental ideas we hold, was not invented by a solitary genius back in the dim recesses of time. We now know the idea of the wheel slowly evolved from one of the most basic industries of our primitive ancestors—the making of pots. Fashioning them from wet clay, the potter had constantly to rotate them to make them round. Slowly the idea of rotating a slab on which the pot stood rather than the pot itself came into use. Following that came a device to rotate the slab with a vertical shaft through its center and a foot pedal to operate it, and lo, the potter's wheel was "invented." But in point of fact the idea had evolved very slowly over a very long period of time. The next step in the process, turning the potter's wheel on its side with the shaft through its center, now horizontal, and adding another disc at the other end of the shaft, also evolved over a long period of time, as did the later stages when the wheel and shaft (axle) together formed the basis for a cart. In each case, however, the new development, once achieved, was quickly copied and its use became widespread.

Scientists agree that the driving force of science is the excitement of discovery, the breaking through into new knowledge and understanding. The same conviction is central in Liberalism when the concept is carried through to its full implications. If in science, and in virtually every other human activity the critical mind asks, why not in religion? C. S. Peirce, the late-nineteenth-century American philosopher whose seminal thinking is only now coming to be fully appreciated, coined a word for the goal of exploration at the highest and/or deepest levels. He suggested *musement* to describe it; musing, we might say, deriving the term from a word already extant. Peirce's musement was a state of free, unrestrained imagining and speculating, a state of mind difficult to achieve, attained by very few people, and then only seldom even by those privileged few.

Conceptualizing

Questing proceeds largely by conceptualizing: thinking up new ideas, bigger, broader, more profound and more comprehensive than those we already have. Such ideas come slowly, however. A genuinely new concept does not suddenly burst upon us as if someone had just turned on the light in a dark room. New ideas come to us imperceptibly, like the dawn.

There is no experience quite like that of the dawn. Out in the country, away from the lights of civilization, it is really dark at night. Except for the stars, and the moon, perhaps, the darkness is complete. If the clouds are heavy it is totally dark. When the dawn comes you do not see it at first. You sense it. But moments later, you become aware of a change in the sky—not light, exactly, but the promise of light, a promise that comes true while you watch.

Roger Penrose, Oxford University mathematician, believes that new ideas come to us in that manner. "The feeling one has when one does mathematical research is far from what the lay person thinks," he observed in an interview following the publication of his *Emperor's New Mind*. "Really very little of it depends on calculation. . . . When it gets to the point where it depends on calculation, you're almost finished." Penrose's mood is close to what religious people call mystical when he talks about the formulation of new mathematical concepts. "I have a feeling that I'm seeing something that is there already," he once remarked. "I've been very Platonic in my view of mathematics for a long time. . . . I'm sure the feeling is very close to what Plato had." Conceptual ideas are of fundamental importance, Penrose asserts unequivocally.[4]

Douglas Hofstadter, author of *Gödel, Escher and Bach,* describes conceptualizing as a process of moving by metaphors. We go from what we already know or understand to ideas we are just beginning to grasp, he says. The idea of the concept is itself a metaphor. It is a protoscientific term awaiting explication. Making variations on a theme with which we are already familiar is the way to go about it. Making such variations is the crux of creativity, he says. So, too, say the people of the new paradigm for religion.

From Fixed to Fluid Concepts

Defenders of traditional religion often charge the critical mind with being unable to see the mystical aspect of things. The demand for testing and checking seems to them to be needlessly picayune and fault-finding. Inquirers, they feel, are too concerned with the discovery of flaws in old-line religion.

There is, however, no inconsistency between critical thinking and the use of a wide-ranging imagination. Quite the opposite: let imagination roam free, says the open mind. Questing is as central as testing in the new paradigm for religion. But when our flights of fancy are over and the imaginative story is told, let us be clear as to what has happened. When we have heard a story that may prove true but as yet is still in the realm of fancy we need to be on our guard. Danger lies in the use to which the results of imaginative thinking may be put. Both careful checking and wide-ranging imagination are required. In our enthusiasm over the beauty of a vision let us not forget that it was only a vision. If we are later to build our lives upon it we have first to test it for validity and then to corroborate our judgment with that of other dispassionate minds.

The shift in our religious thinking for which the inquiring mind calls is not what the traditionalists usually suppose it is. It is not from older theological ideas to new and better ones. The shift the critical mind seeks is from the belief that theological ideas are fixed and permanent to the belief that they can vary, do vary, and that they should vary. The inquiring mind insists that theological ideas grow, change and develop as all idea systems do. In the new paradigm for religion the goal is not agreement on a new and improved set of theological principles. That may be the result, but the goal is the acceptance of a more basic idea: that theological formulations can differ, and should be expected to differ, and that they grow and change. Theological principles require open and free debate and they develop and improve as a result of it.

For those who are steeped in the Judeo-Christian tradition in which belief in dogma and tradition are central, the idea of unity based upon growing, changing concepts rather than on the doctrines themselves is difficult to accept. The university tradition in the West offers a helpful analogy here. Our universities are united not by agreement on what they teach, but on their mutual commitment to the standards by which the body of knowledge they teach is accumulated. There is no enforced agreement as to what that body of knowledge should contain. The agreement is on the standards by which its validity is tested. Agreement as to what that knowledge consists in may be widespread but if not, even if the content of that knowledge is widely divergent as to detail, there is no cause for concern. The same thing is true in the new paradigm for religion. For the inquiring mind unity is achieved through agreement on the importance of questing and testing; agreement not on the results we attain, but on the need to establish stern requirements by which to attain them.

Notes

1. A. N. Whitehead, *Adventures of Ideas* (New York: The Macmillan Co., 1935), p. 332.

2. Ibid., p. 29.

3. Daniel J. Boorstin, *The Discoverers* (New York: Random House, 1983), p. xv.

4. Roger Penrose, in an interview following publication of *The Emperor's New Mind, New York Times*, November 19, 1989.

7

Never Resting

Testing means engaging in a continuous, ongoing process. So, too, does questing. To begin asking questions, not only about what is known, but also about the not yet known, launches us on an endless quest. Every answer to every question reveals yet another question lying beyond it, and beyond that, yet another and another and so on. Testing and questing are the two essential ingredients in the pursuit of knowledge and understanding to which we must now add a third—that the process is continuous. We must keep at it: testing, questing, never resting.

Our Native Conservatism

The notion that we must continually test our knowledge runs counter to one of our most deep-seated human needs. We humans are possessed of a strong urge to keep things stable and in order. For this reason every cultural movement tends to harden, solidify, and become immobile. The art of ancient Egypt is as good an example as one could find. Springing almost instantaneously into full flower in the early Old Kingdom period (the first half of the third millennium B.C.E.) Egyptian art soon became fixed. It remained virtually immobile for some three thousand years thereafter. As late as the Roman period, the first, second, and third centuries C.E., the Egyptians themselves and their Roman masters in Egypt as well were still slavishly following the art forms that had evolved three millennia earlier, when Egyptian civilization was first taking form in the Nile Valley.

The tendency we see so clearly in ancient Egyptian art marks every aspect of religion. Our very human desire is to get things right and then to keep them that way. Growth and change are all very well but when at last we feel we have things in order, our attitude changes. Then we do everything we can to keep them just as they are. As the Egyptians at the beginning of the Fourth Dynasty (ca. 2613 B.C.E.) began consciously to fix the style and technique of funerary wall painting, so religious leaders in virtually all times and places have tended to establish patterns of theology and forms of worship, sacred texts and institutions as permanently as they could. Our social institutions, in particular those that are religious, are under intense pressure toward stabilization at the hands of the authorities who govern them. That is what establishment in religion means. Change threatens authority. It upsets the order authority establishes by which to stabilize an institution and to maintain the authority of its leaders. Unfortunately, the results of achieving establishment have often been more tragic than beneficial. It has meant that religion, which should be the leading force for social improvement, has been almost everywhere and at almost all times the leading force for keeping things as they are, thus sustaining unjust, even immoral social institutions, slavery in the southern United States being a blatant example.

What is true of human institutions is no less true of human idea structures. To be sure, they are much more subtle and therefore more fragile. Patterns of thought flourish for a time, then die out only to be rediscovered later, sometimes over and over again. When our native human urge to reason and reflect, to explore and to inquire meets our equally strong tendency to keep things as they are, we humans seem to be willing to reject new ideas, even when they appear to be beneficial. This was Thomas Kuhn's point. It explained for him and for most of the rest of us the nature of the revolutions that have occurred in scientific thinking, and why they were often slower in coming than we might have expected.

In the new paradigm for religion the same tendency toward an unbending stability is seen in religion, and all possible measures are taken to guard against it. The open mind opposes fixed thought and practice in religion and the open heart opposes the tendency to exclusiveness—the view that you and your group are the elect. Old time religion thinks of its doctrine and practice as too sacred to change.

The religion of the open mind and heart thinks of religion as too sacred *not* to change—constantly, and for the better. The tradition of testing and questing in religion came into existence because the older ecclesiastical institutions were not receptive to testing the old or to questing for the new. Human thought moves on; so must religious thought. James Russell Lowell wrote:

> Time makes ancient good uncouth.
> They must upward still, and onward,
> Who would keep abreast of truth.[1]

The origins of religion in the new as against the old paradigm reside here, in the profound need of the religions to reverse their attitude toward change. The open, inquiring mind urges upon traditional religion the importance of rejecting the ancient idea of fixity in doctrine and practice and of exchanging it for the ideal of fluidity. The open heart urges upon traditional religion the importance of rejecting the ancient idea of election and of replacing it with inter-communication, cooperation, and mutual support among the religions. Humanity must come to terms with the fact of human creativity in religion. Criticism of the old and introduction of the new are human constants. Stifled for a time, they can be counted on to reappear, we know not when or where. But reappear they will. When they do, disruption of old and established ways will follow, destructively so if we try to suppress them.

Change in Traditional Religion

Does traditional religion oppose all change? By no means. The fact that beliefs evolve in traditional religion can easily be documented. As an example one need only turn to the Hebrew Bible and compare it with Jewish theological writing today to see how far contemporary beliefs have departed from the plain meaning of the words as originally written. A full-page advertisement in the *New York Times* in 1983 openly advocated the policy of reinterpreting ancient sacred words. The advertisement was sponsored not by a liberal or radical group, but by the Jewish Theological Seminary of America, which called itself in the notice "The Academic Center of Conservative Judaism."[2]

In Protestantism, keeping the authority of ancient Scripture while interpreting it for modern use has long been advocated. We must cease struggling with the literal meaning of the text, the argument runs. Our task is to reinterpret the old words for our use today. Struggling with the Christmas story in Matthew and Luke, for example, we are urged to seek out their true meaning. The nativity stories are ways in which Christian truth was once expressed, we are told, even if we no longer find them historically valid.

As for the problem of downright unbelievable and distasteful passages in the Bible, some writers have openly advocated the use of "productive imagination." Others would have us simply pass by distasteful or unbelievable passages. Yet others advise us to search out the themes, patterns, and structures by which true Bible meaning is communicated. Dwell on those deeper meanings, they say, not on the literal interpretations which so often give us trouble.

In one way or another, religion must always deal with the tension between the old and the new. Traditional religion, no less than religion in the new paradigm, sees the need and the inevitability of growth and change. Both deal with it according to their best insights into the problem. The difference is really one of pace. But that difference is so great as to amount to a difference in kind. In the new paradigm, religion does not try to keep ancient traditions and ancient Scriptures intact. Openly and purposefully it institutes reform wherever and whenever it is needed. The present glacial pace of reform supported by the traditionalists will not save religion, but will destroy it. Religious thought and practice must move with the culture of which it is a part. In the new paradigm, the thought structures of religion and culture are the same. There is no disjunction between them. Both actively pursue a course of growth and development which involves constant change.

As Far As Knowledge and Conscious Reason Will Go

Must we go on testing and questing forever? Are there no limits to it, no end of the process? Early in this century Gilbert Murray answered that question as well as anyone has. At the end of his *Four Stages of Greek Religion,* published in 1913 before the outbreak of World War I, he sighed, almost audibly, "I confess it seems strange to me as I write here, to reflect that at this moment many of my friends and most of my fellow creatures are, as far as one can judge, quite confident that they possess supernatural knowledge. As a rule, each individual belongs to some body which has received in writing the results of a divine revelation. I cannot share in any such feeling. . . . As far as knowledge and conscious reason will go, [I believe] we should follow resolutely their austere guidance. When they cease, as cease they must, we must use as best we can those fainter powers of apprehension and surmise and sensitiveness by which, after all, most high truth has been reached as well as most high art and poetry; careful, always ready to seek for truth and not for our own emotional satisfaction, careful not to neglect the real needs of men and women through basing our life on dreams; and remembering above all to walk gently in a world where the lights are dim and the very stars wander."[3]

In an earlier chapter, describing the flourishing of primitive mystical religions in ancient Rome, Murray had written: "A great foreign religion came like water in the desert to minds reluctantly and superficially enlightened but secretly longing for the old terrors and raptures from which they had been set free."[4]

Clearly, Gilbert Murray was here drawing a parallel and sounding a warning for our own time. In the foregoing passage he was calling us to high religion based upon the clarity of thought toward which the Western intellectual tradition leads when applied to religion. He was not consciously attempting to summarize the religion of the Western intellectual tradition; he was only expressing his own deep feelings resulting from an intensive study of the classics and his reflections on life in the perspective of what he had learned. Yet, what Murray stated so clearly nearly a century ago amounts to a capsule summary of the open-minded, open-hearted approach to religion that has been evolving in the West. That tradition, born in ancient Greece, emerging again in Western Europe in the Middle Ages, nurtured in the growing universities of the West, and in turn nurturing them, and coming to full flower in the Enlightenment, is the religion of the Western intellectual tradition, the religion of the open mind and heart, the new paradigm for religion. Its goal is truth—knowledge and understanding—thoroughly tested, clearly and unequivocally stated, carrying within itself the power to persuade. The pursuit of that goal never ends.

Notes

1. James Russell Lowell, "The Present Crisis," *Hymns for the Celebration of Life*, ed. Arthur Foote II (Boston: Beacon Press, 1964), p. 168.

2. Advertisement: Jewish Theological Seminary, *New York Times*, 14 September 1983.

3. Gilbert Murray, *The Five Stages of Greek Religion* (Boston: Beacon Press, 1951), p. 171. This is the revised edition of *Four Stages of Greek Religion* (1913).

4. Ibid., p. 143.

8

No Exceptions

Because we humans are fallible creatures, we have continually to test everything we suppose ourselves to know. Because we have wide-ranging curiosity and imagination, in addition to being fallible, we are also continually reconceptualizing what we suppose ourselves to know. We avidly construct new paradigms by which to try to comprehend all the knowledge we have accumulated. We go even further and strive to reach into new realms of understanding where we have never been before. All this we do in the interest of truth-seeking.

One further requirement has now to be added to the three of testing, questing, never resting, if we are to be confident that the knowledge and understanding we have achieved is as valid as we can make it. That requirement is that there are to be no exceptions to the foregoing three standards.

Revelation

On the face of it, one would suppose that the need to meet the four foregoing standards would not be questioned. Not so. In religion, it is often argued, the ordinary rules do not apply; religion is unique; when we are dealing with Deity we *know* Truth. What God has revealed to us need not, should not, cannot be questioned, the traditionalists argue. In religion we need *not* test for Truth nor need we seek it. The basic Truth our religion teaches is already in our possession. In religion, they hold, Truth is ours by revelation.

Ancient and modern, Christian and non-Christian, prophetic and ecclesiastical, the theologies of the multiple religions of humanity still today are built on the belief that God for his/her own purposes breaks into the human consciousness and/or human history from time to time so that his/her will may be known and followed here on earth. Revelation, direct and indirect, is the means by which such knowledge comes to us, according to the traditionalists. We, the humble creatures of earth, are able really to *know* through revelation what otherwise we could not know. We know this by faith.

The contrast between the traditional approach to matters of belief and that of the inquirer is nowhere more vivid than on this issue. Inquirers hold that in religion, as in all things, fundamental knowledge does not come to us by revelation, it comes to us as a result of our pursuit of knowledge and understanding here on earth. Traditionalists rely on revelation, inquirers on inquiry.

The idea of revelation is one of the oldest we humans possess. In early times it was taken for granted that gods, spirits, and demons of every sort interfered in human affairs in almost every conceivable way. That included speaking to individuals directly, as when God spoke to Adam in the Garden of Eden, to Moses on Mt. Sinai, and later on to the prophets according to the Hebrew Bible. In ancient times divine interference in human affairs was thought of in quite specific terms. Reread Homer. Recall the plight of the Greek and Trojan warriors as the gods on Mt. Olympus continually broke into their struggle on the plains of Troy and determined the outcome of their various battles and single combat encounters.

In the religious lore of the ancient Hebrews, as we read it in the Jewish and Christian Bibles of today, Jahweh's revelation of his will to the prophets of Israel is as specific as one could wish. The report of Jahweh's directions to Moses on Mt. Sinai in Exodus and the reports of his revelation of his will to Amos, Hosea, Isaiah, Jeremiah, and the lesser prophets are among the most explicit and best known examples. The Ten Commandments are not the words of Moses according to the Bible text; they are God's own words reported to the people of Israel by Moses as God himself revealed them.

Can Revelation Be Exempted from Testing?

Ancient and honored as it is, the doctrine of revelation, on its face, is an astonishing one. No other discipline—only religion—rests the validity of its teachings on anything approaching so remarkable an idea. Today we fail to appreciate its extravagance because the idea has been with us so long. Almost all of us, when we were still very young, were taught by our elders that God reveals his will to us in various ways, at various times, and we accepted it as we accepted most of the things we were taught before the habit of questioning was formed.

The logic of the doctrine is simplicity itself. If a revelation is genuine, it is divine in origin. If it is divine in origin it is true and valid beyond all doubting. If it is not true, it cannot have been divine. Truth is not temporary. What is true today has always been true and will always be.

Of course every claim by every person to have enjoyed celestial illumination is not accepted in traditional religion. Such claims are carefully examined and their authenticity is established only after the most careful scrutiny. But the idea of revelation itself is not tested. The reports of revelations descending to us from ancient times are not questioned. The concept that revelation of the divine will has often occurred in the past and will occur from time to time in the future is not questioned as we question other ideas—those of Copernicus and Galileo, for example—because the ancient sacred texts are believed to be divine revelations. Recently contradicted by the rapidly accumulating studies of the biblical archeologists, the revelatory character of the texts still is not doubted by believers.

To ask that an alleged revelation be tested for validity may therefore seem inappropriate to religious traditionalists. To check it out regardless of its hallowed and sacred status may be denounced as irreverent, even blasphemous. And yet the inquirer would ask, what is revelation but a human experience? Clearly those to whom such experiences come are certain that theirs are experiences of the Almighty. They are accepted as direct and immediate experiences of God. But it is a fallible human being—one of us—who has these experiences. Regardless of the divine source from which the revelations have supposedly come, the rest of us get them secondhand. A report by a fallible human being is not necessarily a revelation from almighty God; it is at most a report of an individual personal experience. It may or may not be accurate; it may be false in detail or in toto. Who can say?

The question that is asked by the inquiring mind regarding revelation concerns reliability. It is not: What is appropriate? It is rather: Should we make an exception of this claim because of its place at the center of the religions of our culture? In the new paradigm for religion we have no choice. To except religion from testing is not to set it free but to emasculate it.

Inquirers hold that the world desperately needs a religion that can command the allegiance of people, motivate them to righteousness, self-discipline, and high intellectual endeavor. A religion anchored to untested knowledge is powerless to move people steeped in the Western intellectual tradition. But religion can once again draw humanity on to heights it has not heretofore achieved if it will give up its claim to be an exception to the standards of truth-seeking which are central to Western culture. Such is the position of the university tradition in religion.

Revelation is Not What You Thought

The traditionalists, of course, understand very well the problems thoughtful people have with the doctrine of revelation. Their writings attempting to explain and justify the doctrine of revelation are voluminous. Among the best of them is a book published over fifty years ago by H. Richard Niebuhr, a professor at the Yale Divinity School, in which he addressed full-scale the problems involved in the idea. Essentially his solution, which has since gained wide acceptance, was to find new meaning in the term "revelation." It is God disclosing himself, Niebuhr wrote in his *Meaning of Revelation* (1941).

In the new paradigm for religion, there is no reason to oppose the redefining of familiar terms. It is in this way that thought progresses. Our ideas grow and change. Concepts widen and deepen.

In the new paradigm for religion the problem here is that of clarity. In redefining old and familiar terms we can all too easily hide a shift in our pattern of thought. When we keep old beloved words but redefine them, we are very apt to keep old beloved meanings as well, resorting to the new meaning only when hard pressed in a theological argument.

As we usually understand it, revelation is the communicating of divine truth. It comes to us humans when the Divine enters our human thinking. Through revelation we know something we would not know had not that intervention taken place. What we know as a result of a revelation we know because God chose to reveal it to us—so the familiar concept runs.

Niebuhr's redefinition is of little help to contemporary-minded people who are baffled by the older, more familiar idea. If a revelation is God disclosing himself, what God is disclosed? By the time that question is answered, a whole new theology has been developed. Niebuhr's definition shifts the argument from the idea of revelation to the idea of God, one of the oldest and most basic concepts to have formed in the human mind. None is more universal, and none is more pervasive in our thinking. Niebuhr's redefinition of God takes us off the track. The question we were on was neither the existence nor the the nature of deity. We are concerned with the validity of religious belief—specifically the validity of our belief in revelation. Our question is: can any of the doctrines of traditional religion claim exemption from testing and questing? That includes the doctrine of revelation. The human claim to have been privileged to enjoy direct communication with the Almighty, the inquirer insists, is as liable to error as any, perhaps more liable than most. If we are to believe anything so basic or profound, we have to believe basically and profoundly that our belief is valid.

Revelation and Illusion

To begin asking questions about an accepted position of any kind is to step into quicksand. Each step leads us inexorably on. Each question we ask leads to another beyond it. Defenders of traditional faith find this to be true when they concede, as most of them do, that not every revelation from God that people claim to have had is valid. Alleged revelations have to be sorted out rigorously. All prophets are not true prophets. Some prophets suffer from illusions and some supposed prophets turn out to have been deceivers. It is very important that we are able to tell the difference.

The problem of distinguishing between true and false revelations goes back at least as far as ancient Israel. It is raised by implication in the book of Amos and is explicit as early as Jeremiah. "An appalling and horrible thing has happened in the land," he cried on one occasion. "The prophets prophesy falsely."[1] In Matthew's gospel Jesus is reported to have had great concern with the problem of false prophets. The book is replete with dire warnings against being led astray by them.[2]

The dilemma posed by the false prophet haunts every faith that has ever appeared. How do you distinguish them from the true prophets? It is one of the issues which believers, whoever they are, constantly confront with regard to their faith. The most conservative religionists check their faith, just as the inquirers do. They, too, test it constantly. They explain it and defend it by all the canons of validity and consistency that can be found.

The difference between the traditionalists and the inquirers comes at the point where the questioning stops and the answers begin. For the inquirer, once the questioning has begun you cannot suddenly stop your questioning and begin to believe. Once the questioning has begun, it can be stopped only when the last question has been asked, only when every test of the validity of what you are saying has been made, and only when the quest for the adequacy of your statement has been pushed to the outermost limits to which human thought can go. For the inquirer the idea of revelation is so bold and so daring an idea that we dare not entertain it until it has been tested to that degree. A revelation may be God disclosing himself, as H. Richard Niebuhr says, but that idea does not tell inquirers what they want to know. On the fallible human scene where we dwell, inquirers want to know why any statement by anyone is to be relied upon. That includes declarations by those who sincerely believe that God has revealed to them things the rest of us might like to know but do not.

Truth by Proclamation

One of the ways in which traditionalists assert a position of privilege in the Temple of Truth is simply to proclaim what they believe the

Truth to be. They called it "bearing witness" to the truth that is in you. Supporting arguments and evidence are left out. They are regarded as unnecessary. You need merely to declare forthrightly what you believe. That is enough. A striking example of this kind of thinking occurred at the Harvard Divinity School in 1975. David R. Williams, a student graduating in the Master of Theological Studies program, invited to participate in the Baccalaureate service, took the opportunity publicly to accuse the startled faculty of "knowing many words and facts and theories. But they have forgotten what the problem is," Williams continued. "They have forgotten what should make them different from their colleagues in the College: that in the words of the prophet, it is the Fear of the Lord that is the beginning of wisdom." Quoting Jonathan Edwards, he continued, "No degree of speculative knowledge of things of religion is any sure sign of saving grace."[3]

Williams concluded his bold utterance by going back to Martin Luther. " 'Yea 'tis naught if thou quiz thy five senses . . . or take counsel with thy mind or wisdom. But thou must set aside sense and consider 'twere somewhat *other* that makes a Christian. . . .' " Williams then added a final word of his own. "Take the facts you have learned at Harvard," he said, "and use them when you can. But remember that all these answers are only hope, nothing more. The Truth lies beyond, outside ourselves, and that is our salvation." By the "Truth" it is clear that he meant the Christian revelation as understood by evangelical Christianity.

Williams's Harvard Baccalaureate is not an isolated instance, a solitary aberration in which traditional religion declares itself to be in possession of absolute Truth. Many a devout believer, it seems, has experienced a similar conflict between faith and reason. Their solution of the problem has been the same as Williams: to bypass the testing process and go directly to that which they believe to be beyond the limits of the human mind. For Williams it was "the fear of the Lord" and "truth outside ourselves." For others it has been "justification by grace" and "justification by God's undeserved love." It is held that a leap of faith can take us to ultimate Truth that otherwise we could never attain. All follow the well-worn path of Karl Barth and John Henry Newman, of Jonathan Edwards and Martin Luther, of Augustine, and the Apostle Paul. All alike hold to the ancient doctrine of revelation according to which basic knowledge is attained by faith.

All alike believe that we know by faith the truth of revelations held and reaffirmed through the ages in the Judeo-Christian tradition.

In asking questions about the validity of alleged revelations, inquirers do not deny the centrality of the God idea in religion. In no way do they deny the importance of deep conviction in religion. Genuine commitment and profound conviction are its essence. Inquirers would add, however, that for them profound conviction and total commitment are possible only after a thorough testing of the validity of one's convictions and commitments has taken place, with no exceptions allowed for any reason.

In traditional religion there is much talk about our human finitude. Traditionalists continually remind us that we are mortal and subject to all the limitations that go with our finite condition. If that is true, the religion of the open mind and heart asks, how are we able to know in religion what, in other areas of human activity, we would readily concede that we cannot know? How are our human limitations overcome in religion? The inquirer would say: the question is not, can God overcome our human fallibility? It is: How do we overcome our fallibility when we talk about God?

Notes

1. Jeremiah 5:20.
2. For example, Matthew 7:15-20.
3. David R. Williams, *Harvard Divinity Bulletin* (October 1975): 2.

9

The Open Encounter of Mind with Mind

Still pressing on, frustrated, eager to begin stating the beliefs of the new paradigm for religion, we ask: Are we not now ready? Have we not at last set the standards we require? Yes, presumably all this has been accomplished. Then the next step is to frame our basic beliefs in language. It is to state the faith of the new paradigm for religion in simple subject and predicate sentences, with all the ambiguity we can identify drained out and all the hidden assumptions exposed and eliminated. How are we to go about it? Is the manner in which we do it important? Those in the Enlightenment tradition hold that how we go about the business of drawing up our statements of belief is of fundamental importance.

In the previous chapter we saw that creed-making is neither a solitary nor a onetime exercise. It takes place over time and the result is seldom if ever the work of one person. Such writings—the Jewish Torah, the Christian New Testament, Buddhist and Hindu sacred texts—all are composite works. With some exceptions—e.g., various of the letters ascribed to the Apostle Paul—the sacred books of the religions are the result of the interactions of many people over a long period of time. The new paradigm for religion holds that this practice is valid. All who wish to try their hand at the formulation of doctrine should be encouraged to do so. Furthermore, anyone at any time should be encouraged to propose improvements in existing formulations of beliefs. Those who oppose the reformulation of an existing belief system should be given ample opportunity to participate in the ensuing debate as to whether or not the proposed changes are sound.

91

The people who have chosen the open mind and heart as their way in religion ask: What other procedure is possible for us? Admittedly we are fallible creatures. Which of us can suppose that his or her formulation, however satisfactory it may seem, is so sound that no one may properly challenge it? Finite in nature, limited in insight and in reasoning power as we all are, what choice do we have but to engage in open discussion? What can we do other than reach out to everyone else for help, correction, corroboration, amplification, or even the rejection of what we propose if our thinking appears to be unsound.

To have confidence that we are on the right track in what we are saying, we need to have the wisest and most dispassionate of our associates say that they see things as we do, if that is indeed what they see. We need even more to have the wisest and most dispassionate of the people we know point out errors of fact or of judgment in what we are saying, to spot important omissions, and to suggest further elaborations that had not occurred to us.

Only then can we hope to formulate beliefs that are valid and that will serve us religiously. Only then shall we be able to formulate beliefs we can really believe because nothing more persuasive can be found. Beyond that, if, having heard all the objections people have raised, we can still believe we are right, we must continue to argue for and to defend what we have said. The ultimate goal is not agreement; it is the most accurate statement we can make. We are encouraged and sustained by the support of others, but it is only a means to the end we seek. The end is neither victory nor agreement; it is validity. The goal is truth, or as close as we can come to stating it.

Freedom of Thought and Expression

We are talking about another basic principle discovered, stated, and fought over by the ancient Greeks. As questing, testing, and never resting are central principles of the new paradigm for religion, so, too, is the freedom to do it. That means believing in full and complete freedom of thought and expression. A partial test is without meaning. An arrested quest is empty. In the absence of freedom the inquiring mind in religion disintegrates, its most essential ingredient nullified. Maximum validity in the formation of beliefs can be achieved only when everyone is free to explore to the uttermost every proposition that is offered and to point out whatever shortcomings may be found in it. In the new paradigm for religious freedom full, untrammeled, and complete discussion is seen as the indispensable means to this end.

The first explicit statement of this doctrine came at the hands of Socrates only a little over a century after Thales' time. We owe to Socrates and to his spokesman Plato a verbatim report of his glowing words. In the *Apology* Plato reports Socrates as saying: "I go about the city, testing your opinions and trying to show you that you are really ignorant of what you suppose you know. Daily discussion of the matters about which you hear me conversing is the highest good. . . . Life that is not tested by such discussion is not worth living. . . . If you acquit me . . . upon condition that I may not inquire and speculate anymore . . . I shall reply [that I] honor and love you but I shall obey God rather than you, and while I have life and strength I shall never cease from the practice and teaching of philosophy. . . . I cannot hold my tongue. Daily discussion about virtue and those other things about which you hear me examining myself and others is the greatest good. . . . The unexamined life is not worth living."[1]

The principle is not confined to religion; it is universal in its application. Justice Oliver Wendell Holmes stated it in one of his Supreme Court opinions in his usual lucid style, "When men have realized that time has upset many fighting faiths, they may come to believe even more than they believe the very foundations of their own conduct that the ultimate good desired is better reached by free trade in ideas—that the best test of truth is the power of the thought to get itself accepted in the competition of the market, and that truth is the only ground upon which their wishes safely can be carried out. That, at any rate, is the theory of our Constitution. It is an experiment, as all life is an experiment."[2]

This being the human condition, say the people of the new paradigm for religion, it applies to religion, as to all things. Our task is to gather as much information as we can that bears upon the decisions we have to make. Only through the participation of a wide variety of people, and only through minds and hearts and spirits that are truly open to one another can we attain the best possible statement. Our goal can be nothing less than that.

During Senator Joseph McCarthy's witchhunts of the 1950s, Learned Hand, another great American jurist, declared, "I believe that the community is already in a process of dissolution where faith in the eventual supremacy of reason has become so timid that we dare not enter our convictions in the open lists, win or lose. . . . Mutual confidence on which all else depends can be maintained only by an open mind and a brave reliance upon free discussion."[3] The new paradigm for religion would insist that the principle applies no less to religion than to the law.

The doctrine of freedom is multifaceted and subtle. Freedom is not an absolute good, always to be desired, never limited in any way. Freedom is the means to high purpose; it is not an end in itself. I am not free to hit someone in the face. I am not free to rob other people of their freedom. In religion these same principles hold. Religion does not remove the limits to which liberty must always be subjected.

One of the major aspects of human thought that often goes unnoticed is the spirit of cooperation and mutual assistance it engenders. Thought is inherently democratic. Except when we are inhibited by custom or authority, we spontaneously share our thoughts with one another. For the sheer joy of it we tell other people about new ideas that occur to us. By our interaction with them our thoughts are clarified and we are stimulated to think further. When we try out on others things we have been mulling over, their puzzled reaction to our words often enables us to see more clearly what we have in mind. For sound thinking we are indispensable to one another.

In the new paradigm for religion, the structures we build for its operation must not only permit the full and free exchange of ideas, they must go further and encourage it, stimulate it, in fact arrange for it. Not only do the protagonists in a theological encounter learn from one another, often they borrow from one another, frequently without being aware of it. When an encounter is really open, the protagonists tend to grow together if they strive to understand their opponents while making their own positions clear.

The silent acceptance of Enlightenment ideas by their orthodox critics is a case in point. So, too, is the clash between religion and science in the nineteenth and twentieth centuries. Both clearly show slow acceptance of Enlightenment ideas by the established religions even as they strove to refute what the Enlightenment was saying.

The growing acceptance of the new paradigm for religion in mainline religion today is only the latest instance of the working of this principle.

The Limits of Free Speech

Those who support the ecclesiastical form of church organization have long held that open interchange among all parties too often leads to acrimonious and unprofitable debate, indecision, inaction, and ultimately fragmentation of the movement. Final authority must rest with the institution, they hold, not with the individual.

They have a point. Little agreement can be expected in a fully open theological forum where ideas of all sorts can be freely exchanged. A striking example is that of the Free Religious Association, a splinter group that developed among the American Unitarians in the second half of the nineteenth century. The movement began among the Transcendentalists, who were opposing a Unitarian drift back toward a middle-of-the-road liberal Christianity that set in following the Civil War. They withdrew from the Unitarian Association in a dual protest, first against what they saw as an infringement on their right to freedom of expression, and second because they wanted to meet in an atmosphere that they believed would be more congenial to the expression of novel theological views.

The Free Religious Association ended as a debating society, destroyed rather than liberated by the doctrine of freedom of speech. The majority of the members, fearful lest a full and open exchange of ideas be limited in some way, defeated every positive proposal brought before the meetings of the society. They insisted that all who wished to speak should be heard. That in turn required the entire body to sit and listen while anyone who chose to, spoke his or her mind. The Free Religious Association foundered on the doctrine of freedom, the limits of which they seem not to have understood. The Association ultimately disintegrated under the impact of its own noncredal dogma.

Who is to blame when one person in a gathering, large or small, consumes too much time, expressing his/her ideas? On such an occasion it is the chairperson more than the talker who is to blame. A presiding officer committed to full freedom of expression needs to see that the excessive talker is in effect denying to all others the right to be heard and doing so as effectively as any censor might. A presiding officer who lets a person talk on and on does not affirm but denies freedom of speech. The principle is the same in religion, politics, board meetings, or committee work. For freedom of speech to be real, there must be limits on the time any one speaker takes. Apparently the Free Religious Association never quite grasped this principle.

Many limitations on freedom of speech are required in order to maintain true freedom. For example, need we grant such freedom to the anarchist or the fascist who would use freedom of speech to advocate abolishing it? Should we grant freedom of speech to perverse minds who want it only to discomfit the rest of us with their obscenities? These are old and familiar questions, and as with many on which we have touched, an extensive literature awaits anyone who cares to pursue the question further. Here we need only observe that freedom of speech will end in clamor or frustration unless it is equally free for all.

Can we maintain full freedom of thought and expression, and also maintain the essential controls on those who would abuse or even destroy it? Few things we humans undertake in organized society are more difficult, yet these are essential in the new paradigm for religion. Cost what it may, no price is too high for genuine freedom of thought and expression.

Bronowski and Mazlish in their *Western Intellectual Tradition* concluded that the great creative ages in Western thought were those in which dissent is welcomed, not suppressed. The societies that provided for the expression of new ideas were the most creative, they asserted. In the democracies of the West, opposition to the government has not been suppressed: it has been legalized and protected, they continued. The balance between power and dissent is the heart of the Western intellectual tradition. In the West we have a tradition of questioning what is traditional. History is made in the conflict of ideas, the conflict of minds. Such is the goal and practice of religion in the new paradigm.

Notes

1. Plato, *Apology,* in *Dialogues of Plato,* vol. 1, trans. Benjamin Jowett (New York: Random House, 1937), p. 419.

2. Oliver Wendell Holmes in *Abrams* v *United States,* 205 U.S. 616 (1919).

3. Learned Hand, Address to the Eighty-sixth Convention, New York University, 24 October 1952.

10

The Open Heart

In the new paradigm for religion belief in freedom, full and free, is central. But the concept is also realistic. It is freedom for all, not for one above another, and often that means restricting my freedom in order that yours can be as great as mine. Being free ourselves must never permit us to get in the way of freedom for someone else. Presumably all of us are equally eager to be free of restraint. At any rate each of us is equally entitled to be.

When the new paradigm for religion sets the doctrine of freedom at the center of its belief structure, it means not only the full and free exchange of ideas in the pursuit of truth in religion; it means no less the full and free exchange of more specifically theological ideas. It means a completely open interchange among the religions of the world and the people organized within them. That means tolerance toward people who worship gods that are strange to us, and tolerance toward people whose values and patterns of conduct are different from ours as well. As the new paradigm for religion holds to the doctrine of the open mind, it holds even more emphatically to the doctrine of the open heart. In the new paradigm for religion respect for religions that are foreign to us is an integral part of our own religion. In the new paradigm we extend to the people of other religions openness, friendliness, and understanding. Our goal is the religion of the open heart no less than that of the open mind.

Intolerance

Virtually all religions, and the sects and groups within them, justify their separate existence doctrinally. They are certain that they possess religious truths that others do not possess. It is their privilege, they believe, to protect those truths, to preach them, to promote them, and to live and worship in accordance with them. The inevitable result is intolerance toward all other religions. All are looked upon as in some sense inferior. This we call intolerance.

The history of religion is the history of intolerance. In religion we find intolerance not only between the organized religions great and small, we find it between the sects and factions that divide most of the religions internally. In Islam there are the Shiites and the Sunnis. In Judaism there are the Orthodox, the Conservative, the Reformed, and the Reconstructionist movements. In Christianity there is the Roman Catholic Church, the Eastern Orthodox Church, Protestantism with its countless denominations and divisions, and outside those structures innumerable sects like the Mormons and Christian Scientists. Beyond all of these are the innumerable new sects, some small and some large and powerful, like the Baha'is, who do not even claim to be Christian. Interreligious hostility seems to be with us still, here in America, even at this late date.

Religion, by nature, is not *inclusive*, it is *exclusive*. Tolerant in its primitive stages perhaps, when spirits were thought to dwell in everything from stars to snakes, the religions and their gods, as they grew in strength and stability, found themselves in competition with one another. As priesthoods developed, as shrines were established, and as temples were built, the deities to whom they were dedicated were seen by their devotees as true gods. All others inevitably were looked on as false. They were seen as idols, not deities. Gods other than their own were dismissed, denounced as pretenders, imposters, and devils.

The Hebrew Bible, the Old Testament for Christians, exhibits this struggle clearly as it took place in Israel. "Thou shalt have no other gods before me," was the first of the Ten Commandments that God delivered to Moses on Mt. Sinai, says Exodus 20:3. The Hebrew Bible, almost from beginning to end, can be read as an expansion of this theme. It resounds through the first five books of the Bible, through Samuel and Kings, and is the constant message of the prophets.

The Coming of Tolerance

Imperial Rome reverted to the earlier, more tolerant approach. The multiple gods of the conquered peoples of the empire were neither denounced nor rejected. Instead their worship was allowed to continue in an atmosphere of genuine tolerance. Christianity was born and spread throughout the empire in this tolerant atmosphere. The Christians found themselves in trouble only when they, in their intolerance, refused to conform to the one exception Rome made in its tolerant position—that the emperor also be worshipped as a deity. Ironically it was the intolerance of the Christians in tolerant Rome that brought upon them the persecutions from which they suffered so much.

The Roman Empire found room not only for the many religions that came with the acquisition of conquered lands, but also for philosophical speculation about the gods. The atomists Democritus and Lucretius; the Cynics Diogenes Laertius, Zeno, and Lucian; the Stoics Seneca, Epictetus, and Marcus Aurelius were read and heard in ancient classical Rome. All were permitted to speak and to criticize one another.

There is a noticeable parallel between these developments in the Roman Empire and our situation today. Ours, too, is a time in which we are learning more than we ever supposed there was to know about strange and different forms of religious belief and practice around the world. Today the news media—television, newspapers, magazines—continually carry stories and pictures about vibrant forms of faith, a great many of them obviously more powerful and persuasive to their adherents than ours are to most of us.

Happily, today the mood in the West, and perhaps worldwide, is changing from intolerance to mutual acceptance. Even in the face of the rising fanaticism in the East, we see today increasing respect for other religions and an increasing interest in learning about them. That means a mutual recognition by the religions of each other's rights. It marks a surprising and to many a very gratifying change from the exclusivity of the past in which each religion claimed preeminence for itself and ascribed second-class status to the rest.

As an example, until very recently, the official position of the Roman Catholic Church was that there is no salvation outside of it. Pope John XXIII gets the credit for the change. His action was symbolized by his inviting to the Second Vatican Council in 1962 thirty-nine "Separated Brethren," from Christian Orthodox, Protestant, and Anglican churches. The name for the end of Roman Catholic exclusivism is "ecumenism," meaning a movement related to the entire body of churches, not only those of one's own group or affiliation. *Nihil obstat*, nothing stands in the way of ecumenism, was the formal declaration of the Second Vatican Council.

The attitude of mutual acceptance and mutual understanding that church bodies today extend to one another carries this spirit even further. Current writers assert that the future of religion lies in their mutual acceptance of one another in true dialog. Hans Küng, the German Roman Catholic thinker, has laid heavy emphasis on this point. Discussing possibilities for dialog with Islam[1] he began by quoting the statement of the Council of Florence in 1442: "The Holy Church of Rome . . . believes firmly, confesses and proclaims that no one outside the Catholic church, neither heathen nor Jew nor unbeliever, nor one who is separated from the Church, will share in eternal life, but will perish in the eternal fire which is prepared for the devil and his angels, if this person fails to join it (the Catholic Church) before death." Küng then went on to say: "Today the traditional Catholic position is no longer the official Catholic position. The Second Vatican Council declared unmistakably in its *Constitution Concerning the Church* that, 'those who through no fault of their own do not know the Gospel of Christ or his Church, but who nevertheless seek God with a sincere heart and, moved by grace, try in their actions to do his will as they know it through the dictations of their conscience— these, too, may achieve eternal salvation' " [Art. 16].

Tolerance was central in the Enlightenment thought pattern. The philosophes of the seventeenth and eighteenth centuries took the lead in insisting that tolerance be established as a stated principle and put into practice in the Christian West. The English Act of Toleration of 1689 is a case in point. It meant establishing toleration officially in England. Previously it had been a crime often punished by death to challenge official Christian doctrine. The tolerance the Act permitted was very limited, to be sure. The importance of the English Act of 1689 lay in the future toward which it pointed, as well as the shameful past it was leaving behind.

Pluralism

In a curious way the world today is moving toward the practical solution of the problem of multiple competing faiths already reached in ancient Rome. People not heretofore advocates of tolerance are beginning to say: let all of the various religions stand, so long as they don't interfere with one another or with society and culture. Let people worship what gods they will and in the manner they deem most appropriate. Only let them not interfere with those who see things differently. Let them be truly tolerant of those who worship "foreign" gods and who preach strange doctrines.

Our name for this state of affairs is "pluralism." The word itself is new. It first appeared in 1818. Initially the usage was not theological but political. "Pluralism" at first meant holding two offices at the same time. But today, in theological circles it has come to mean the coexistence on equal terms of separate competing religious groups. Recognition of this state of affairs may be official or unofficial. Pluralism is found when, as in the United States for example, and many other countries as well, strong, sometimes mutually antagonistic religious groups flourish side by side without interfering with one another's thought or activities.

As it was in ancient Rome, the solution of the problem in our time is as much political as theological. In the United States, for example, pluralism has become a fact of our religious life as a result of the doctrine of the "separation of Church and State." It emerged as a result of the Founding Fathers' determination to eliminate from the new nation the religious wars that had stained the face of Europe for the previous 1500 years or more. In the mid 1900s the theologians began openly to recognize the result of this principle as it had worked out in practice. They called it "pluralism." The Bill of Rights in the American Constitution had not established it officially. But that was its result.

In the United States the doctrine of the separation of church and state was a recognition by the founders of the nation of the importance of such a separation of powers. They saw the difference between theology and philosophy, and wrote it into the Constitution. They did not outlaw either theology or religion. They permitted the continuance of both even when organized in strong and privileged institutions. What the Founding Fathers did was to take from the religions all political power and authority. Power and authority was given to the structures of government. The government, in turn, was to be subject to the will of the people, with everyone guaranteed an opportunity to have their say. As a result, in the United States, where the doctrine of the separation of church and state is clearly established, theological disagreement, often sharp, continues. But it seldom invades the halls of government. To this day, no sect enjoys the official backing of the state.

Must I Give Up My Own Faith?

The idea of pluralism does not solve the problem of conflict and controversy between the established religions, however. That problem was not solved, it was bypassed. Many people are happy to leave things that way. Others are not. They realize that to accept pluralism as the appropriate religious attitude is to accept a kind of double-think situation in which they profess preeminence for their own faith while acting as if none was preeminent and all stood alike in the eyes of the Almighty.

A favorite solution of this problem since Renaissance times has been that of "Many Mansions." The reference is to John's Gospel where Jesus is quoted as saying, "In my Father's house are many mansions."[2] Another metaphor, this one taken from Renaissance writers, is that of many paths up the mountain of truth, where, at last, we all meet at the top. That was the Enlightenment view as well. It is typified in the parable "Nathan the Wise," a poem by Lessing, the eighteenth-century German poet. The point of the parable is the validity to be found in all the religions. This being so, let each strive to prove itself by results is the message of the poem, not with rancor or in armed conflict but with gentleness and heartiest friendliness, with benevolence and true devotedness to God.

Hans Küng believes that today we are "witnessing the slow awakening of global ecumenical consciousness." We are, he says, at "the beginning of a serious religious dialogue between both leading experts and broad-based representatives. . . . Ecumenism should not be limited to the community of the Christian churches," he insists. "It must include the community of the great religions." Küng then goes on to ask a question that is implicit in the pluralist approach. It is a question that is today troubling many Western writers. How is it possible to affirm a true ecumenism and at the same time affirm one's Christian or Jewish or Islamic faith? "I trust that God has acted in history . . . ," Küng replies. "I believe in the Christ who suffered, died and was taken up and now stands on the right hand of God. I attempt to follow him. For me he is *the* way, *the* truth, and *the* light."[3]

Küng advocates the formulation of "fundamental ethical criteria with an appeal to the common humanity of all which rests upon the humanism, the truly human—concretely, on human dignity and the fundamental values inherent in it." He believes this is now going on. In short, his answer is that for him, the central Christian dogma—the Christ—remains preeminent.[4]

Having Your Faith and Ecumenism, Too

And so the question lingers and will not go away. Some theologians, almost in desperation, it seems, give up trying to reconcile irreconcilables and urge a bold, unequivocal declaration of the preeminence of one's own faith. Acknowledge the reality if not the validity of other contrasting faiths, they urge, but then affirm your own. The sharper and clearer statements of our own faith are, they declare, the more readily we understand one another and the more easily we get together. This seeming double-think is accomplished by personalizing one's position. In Küng's words: "Seen from *within*, from the standpoint of a believing Christian . . . *the true religion for me* [is] Christianity, insofar as it bears witness in Jesus to the one true God."[5]

Others have argued that the issue itself is a false one, that where non-Christian religions are valid they are at one with Christian teachings. Thus there is no conflict between them because they hold to the same basic principles. Since long before pluralism was ever heard of, Christians seeking rapport with non-Christian faiths have insisted that Christianity is itself universal. The Christ, properly understood, is a universal, they say. He is not a sectarian figure. But that stance cannot pass the acid test of Jewish or Buddhist or Islamic faith. Those religions and nearly all others would as readily insist that theirs is the universal faith, and that Christians could easily subscribe to it if they cared to.

The "One" is manifest in many ways, a typical argument runs. Each of the religions, in their sacred writings, in their prayers, and in the various means of grace they identify, seeks the One and perceives the One. In the process each of the religions tries to impose its particular set of validating criteria on all the others. Christians of this persuasion find Christ present in Buddhism. Increasingly today, religious leaders find transcending experience present in all religions. Reality is conceived in different ways in the several religions, they say, but that need not separate them from one another. In the end, all who are willing can meet and unite in the common religious experience that transcends all differences.

Some Christian writers have seemingly given up. They would openly acknowledge the fact of deep religious diferences, and they would acknowledge as well the pain that is latent in that situation. The problem is peculiarly Christian, says one writer, because the Christians themselves have divided into so many different sects, each intolerant of all the others, some fiercely so. "Let all the competing groups practice a mutual forgiveness" is his way of dealing with the problem. Unfortunately, however, his is not a solution. It is merely a proposal as to how the various Christian sects might get along with one another.

Martin Marty, church historian and commentator, underscores the point. He asks whether the power of one's personal faith is not lost in the ecumenism or pluralism that prevails, as for example, in academe today, as the various forms of religion in America strive to conform to the university tradition in their teaching while remaining loyal to the stated articles of the faith they profess.

Joining Hands and Hearts

Contemporary-minded people are excited by the growing ecumenical mood of today, but they do not find the theological arguments of the traditionalists very helpful. Imbued with the mind-set of the West, they deeply believe that mutually contradictory bodies of doctrine cannot be the point at which we come to rest. Rather, it must be the point of departure. Contradiction is the place where we set out on the road of discovery.

Unfortunately, after all the arguments are over and all the attempts at reconciliation have been made, the question still stands: how can mutual acceptance among the several religions and loyalty to one's own faith be achieved simultaneously? To choose one is to deny the other. How can a religious group that believes in the uniqueness and the superiority of its teachings concede the equality and validity of another clearly different faith that also thinks of itself as superior and unique? In asserting its claim to hold unique, divinely sanctioned Truth, does not each irretrievably lock itself off from all the rest? On the other hand, does not mutual respect and caring invite each sect to approach all others in openness, in mutual respect and affection? Yet if they do, surely they show themselves to be but weak adherents of their own faith.

The solution to this problem that the religion of the open mind and heart would offer is very simple. It would point out that for at least twenty-five centuries the culture of the West has been moving toward a new mode in religion. Unlike the old, the new mode is not centered in doctrines, dogmas, and traditions descending to us from an ancient and sacred past. It is centered in clear, hard thinking in the present. It is centered in observation, experimentation, reflection, and imagination, rooted in mutual respect and affection for people of differing religious convictions. Religion in this mode has little patience with the claims and counterclaims of the established religions that set them in divisive and frequently bloody conflict with one another.

This is the religion of the open mind and heart. It comes out where Huston Smith came out after a sympathetic, competent, and detailed study of the religions of the world. Smith ended his study with the simple fact of pluralism, although he did not use the term.[6]

When we look at the religions of the world, we find they are not all saying the same thing, he wrote. Yet the number of things they hold in common is large and significant. We find also that all of the truths we believe to be important are not to be found in any one tradition. Most of the things we might like to say about the religions we find we cannot say with total confidence, Smith concludes. There is, however, one thing we can say with total confidence: We must listen to one another. We must do so openly and attentively. We must be ready and eager to learn from one another. This is the position of the religion of the open mind and heart stated flatly and clearly. It is the new paradigm for religion. It requires a mind that is constantly open to new knowledge and a heart that is yet more open to people and to the seemingly infinite variety of beliefs they hold.

Notes

1. Hans Küng, "Christianity and World Religions: The Dialogue with Islam as One Model," *Harvard Divinity Bulletin* (December 1984–January 1985): 4.

2. John 14:2.

3. Hans Küng, "Chrisitianity and World Religions," p. 4.

4. Hans Küng, *Theology for the Third Millennium: An Ecumenical View,* trans. Peter Heinegg (New York: Doubleday, 1988), p. 254.

5. Ibid.

6. Huston Smith, *The Religions of Man* (New York: Harper & Brothers, 1958), p. 309.

11

Uncertainty and Quandary

In chapter 5 we set out to state the beliefs that are to be found in the new paradigm for religion. As yet we have not succeeded in stating any. We have noted the fact of our human fallibility. We have seen the requirement of careful testing and checking whatever we propose to say. We have noted the excitement and the rewards of wide-ranging imagination in our pursuit of truth, the need to be thoroughgoing in what we do, and the need to keep at it. Testing our views in the court of world opinion seems to be the best way to achieve these goals together with an open, appreciative attitude toward those who differ from us.

These are beliefs in the sense that in the new paradigm for religion they are stoutly held to and closely observed. No one doubts their validity. But are they religious beliefs? They are really not so much beliefs as the standards we must meet if truly believable beliefs are to be attained. Credible beliefs can be arrived at, inquirers believe, only after they have been thoroughly tested for accuracy and validity; only after they have been set over against the widest ranging beliefs we can formulate; only when we have pressed our testing and probing to the outermost limits; only when we have made no exceptions to these standards; only after we have invited all the critics in to tell us where they think we are wrong; and only when, with an open heart, we have considered the alternatives offered to us by those with deep faith in a quite different religion.

When we have done all these things; when we have faithfully met every standard; even then, how can we be sure of the truth of the beliefs we would state? The traditional religions assure us of

109

the truth of their teachings through the doctrine of revelation, but we have seen that that doctrine cannot be incontestably established. What better ground does the new paradigm for religion offer on which to rest the authority of its beliefs?

If we begin with the fact of human fallibility and if we rule out revelation, are we not condemned to an ultimate *un*certainty as to the most basic things in life? If so, does it follow that the new paradigm for religion is a paradigm for nothing? Does the new paradigm offer us a new way in religion, or does it consign us to a way out of religion into nihilism?

Uncertainty in Science

Traditionally, religion has been very sure of itself. By virtue of the doctrine of revelation it *knows*, where all others are only groping about, unsure of themselves, without anything solid upon which to anchor. Back in the 1930s, when the Heisenberg Principle of Inde-terminacy first gained prominence, it was hailed by many a theologian as an argument in favor of religion. If science itself is ultimately uncertain about the truth it labors so hard to establish, they argued, then the traditional way in religion is at least as valid as the scientific way. In fact, it is more so, because it has the doctrine of revelation to support its claims. Now uncertain of its own conclusions, science admits that it does not know what religion knows by faith, they said.

In point of fact, however, what Heisenberg had said gave no sup-port whatever to traditional religious teachings. The *Scientific American* pointed this out as soon as such articles began to appear. In the April 1932 issue a news item noted that: "The 'principle of indeterminacy,' has been construed to mean that, as Sir James Jeans puts it, 'nature abhors accuracy and precision above all things. . . .' A. H. Compton, Millikan, Eddington and others of great fame have given encouragement to this idea, and the clergy have not been slow to seize hold of their encouragement. . . . But many physicists seriously question the interpretation being given [the] principle. . . . All [it] means is that man has no way of determining both the position and the speed of a given electron, not that there is no determinancy in either."[1]

In common language, Heisenberg had said: When we deal with

things that are infinitely small, we don't really know whether we are dealing with waves or particles. In that situation the observer becomes a part of what is observed. This is a deduced principle of microphysics. It is not a law of epistemology. Heisenberg had not said that we are forever condemned to uncertainty, even though in fundamental things that may well be our human condition. Kurt Gödel stirred up the same kind of speculation among the clergy when he showed that any complex formal system is inherently flawed. Closely examined, it will be seen to be either incomplete or inconsistent, he said, in what came to be known as his "Incompleteness Theorem."

We need to be clear that neither the principle of indeterminacy nor the incompleteness theorem applies to the ideas with which religion deals in explaining our world or in ordering our lives. Neither principle applies to stories of events in the past which have become the foundation of religious faith. Miraculous tales about what the theologians call "God's mighty acts" are not proved true by either principle. Indeterminacy and uncertainty in science say nothing whatever about the certainty or validity of moral precepts of the religions. Neither do they say anything about their miracles, or about their many widely varying creation stories. The principle of indeterminacy and the incompleteness theorem are not statements about the validity of human knowledge. They are scientific theories only, and they are narrowly confined to the subject matter they address. They pretend to be nothing more. They prove nothing one way or the other about the doctrines and dogmas of religion.

Anyone who would rest a case for religious believing on the thought of either Gödel or Heisenberg should read Raymond Smullyan's *Forever Undecided*.[2] There religious venturers will be set straight in short order. Smullyan's logical puzzles will readily persuade readers that we cannot, by logic alone, reason ourselves to a reliable conclusion. That, he says, is what ails all belief systems. He might well have added, but did not, "and that includes the belief systems of the religions—all of them."

The scientists themselves have made it clear as to where they stand on the issue of certainty and finality of the sort the religions so often claim. Alfred Tarski, the Polish-American mathematician and logician, showed that there is no universal language or system in which we can develop, in a formal way, the ability to say everything that is true. Alfred North Whitehead and Bertrand Russell had tried to reach finality in their *Principia Mathematica*, published in two volumes in 1910 and 1913, only to have it demonstrated soon afterward that the ideal they had in view is unattainable.

Percy Bridgman, the American physicist, also insisted that we can achieve neither objectivity nor certainty in science. A dumb intuition is the closest we can get, he said back in 1959. It is "a feeling in our bones that we know what we are doing."[3] We may wish it might be different, he concluded, but that is the way things are.

What Science Is

The attempt to establish the credibility of religion by pointing out uncertainty in science is old stuff. Why bring all this up again? Because these arguments are still heard today. Our need, however, is not to refute them, but rather to understand what science is and what it is and is not saying. James Bryant Conant, former president of Harvard University, did this for us in 1946 in a series of semi-popular lectures, *On Understanding Science*.

"Science emerges from the other progressive activities of man," he wrote, "to the extent that new concepts arise from experiments and observations and the new concepts, in turn, lead to further experiments and observations." Some concepts are fruitless, he continued, "but others are fruitful. . . . The texture of modern science is the result of the interweaving of fruitful concepts."[4] In 1951, Conant refined his statement to read: "Science is an interconnected series of concepts and conceptual schemes that have developed as a result of experimentation and observation, and are fruitful of further experimentation and observations."[5] The true scientist is interested more in the future, he insists, than in the present. The significant thing is not what science has done but what it is now doing. At about the same time J. Robert Oppenheimer, the atomic physicist, observed that "science is more of a unity of dedication than of understanding."[6]

We can take what Conant and Oppenheimer said two generations ago as authoritative. In various forms their way of stating what science is and does has been repeated continually ever since. Other writers have stressed other aspects of science: the integrity of the scientist, the ever-present possibility of misconception and error in science, the importance of scientific integrity, and of the scientific community as the members interact with one another.

"Science is an investigative enterprise that is faithful to the facts," Jacob Bronowski wrote. "The purpose of science is to discover what is true about the world. . . . We can practice science only if we value truth."[7] The point is fundamental. This is where science and much of fundamentalist religion do not meet but pass each other in the night. It is why the retort "You cannot disprove what we say," so frequently heard among religious conservatives, goes unanswered. "Creationism," for example, may claim to be an alternative to science, but it is not. Scientists reject its theories, not because they disagree but because no means exist by which we can find out whether they are right or wrong.

What Science is Not and What it Does Not Say

In the religion versus science argument we need to understand both the achievements of science and the limits within which it works, as the scientists themselves view the matter. They have been voluble on the question. Here are some of their most succinct and penetrating observations.

"Science shouldn't be seen as a system of belief," Donald Culross Peattie, the botanist, observed in his *Flowering Earth*. "It is rather a way of asking questions of the universe. We have to be ready at all times," he continued, "to scrap the most cherished and appealing theories."[8] The clearest and most succinct statement of the principle I have found lay almost hidden in a book review. It read, "The power and beauty of science do not rest upon infallibility which it has not, but upon corrigibility, without which it is nothing."[9]

Peter Gay, striving as always to make the nature of the Enlightenment clear, pointed out that "The eighteenth-century philosophes wanted to do more than simply understand the world . . . they wanted to change it through understanding it. . . . They were neither foolish optimists nor foolish rationalists. They were people of good will and good hope. . . . They could tolerate uncertainty and unresolved questions. They had no patience with people who demand of science the kind of certainty it cannot give." Quoting Sigmund Freud, Peter Gay added, "Only the real, rare, true scientific minds can endure doubt, which is attached to all our knowledge."[10]

John L. Casti, an applied mathematician at the Technical University of Vienna, devoted a book to the subject of certainty in science. In his *Searching for Certainty* (1991), he asserts that fallibility is an unavoidable aspect of the scientific endeavor. For this reason the kind of certainty for which we humans yearn is not attainable, even in the most exacting scientific endeavor.

This, then, is where we come out. Since we human creatures are fallible, we cannot be certain of the knowledge we have accumulated. Emphasizing this point, Lewis Thomas, research pathologist and medical administrator, said in a Phi Beta Kappa address at Harvard University in 1980: "Uncertainty, the sure sense that the ground is shifting at every step, is one of the marks of humanity. . . . The great body of science, built like a vast hill over the past three hundred years, is a mobile, unsteady structure, made up of solid-enough single bits of information, but with all the bits always moving about, fitting together in different ways. . . . Human knowledge doesn't stay put."[11]

But notice: The human condition of uncertainty, like that of fallibility, is not a religious belief. It is a statement of fact derived from observation. This is how things are. If you doubt it, look around. If you think any thoughtful human being can be absolutely certain of Truth, examine carefully the writings of those who say they can. Examine the authorities on whom they rely. They claim a lot, a *lot*. Look in particular at the questions being asked by the skeptics and doubters. Do the answers of the believers hold up? Does the evidence they offer to support their position do so? Do the arguments they marshall sustain their absolute certainty?

To sum up, the new paradigm for religion is not the religion of science. It does not rest upon scientific findings, and it does not look to the scientific community for the foundation upon which ultimate principles rest. The new paradigm for religion is one with science, however, in the standards it applies in the pursuit of knowledge, understanding, and truth. The standards for this process are those of the Western intellectual tradition, the university tradition, and the religion of the open mind and heart. All alike begin with the fact of our human fallibility and hold to the highest possible standards in an attempt to surmount those limitations as we strive to get into words what the truth really is.

"We live in a cloud of unknowing," wrote an anonymous fourteenth-century Christian thinker, a line much quoted today. For the inquirer, that is the way out of the problem of uncertainty— to see that it isn't a problem for people willing and able to face up to the factual situation in which we humans find ourselves. It is our task to learn to live in a world of ultimate uncertainty. In the new paradigm for religion we are not crushed by the loss of a certainty we never had. We are exhilarated by the discovery of uncertainties because they invite us into a world still to be explored and better understood. Said the London *Economist* in a 1991 editorial, "The triumph of the twentieth century is that it has purged itself of certainty."

Quandary

The pathway we have been following seems to have brought us to a conclusion opposite to the one we sought. It has not brought us to a set of dependable beliefs by which we can understand our universe and live our lives. It has not brought us to the certainties we expect in religion. Instead, we have been brought to ultimate uncertainty. The attempt to state the faith of the new paradigm for religion has brought us to quandary in which there are no beliefs certain enough to be the object of faith.

What to do? To begin with, attacking this problem we discover that there is no word in English for not being certain. We have only the negative "uncertainty." Apparently the condition of uncertainty is not sufficiently pervasive in our thinking to require a name. We have "misery" for *un*happiness, "mess" for *un*tidiness, "intended" or "purposeful" for *un*intended—examples abound. But we have no word for uncertainty except "quandary," which carries the wrong shade of meaning. Synonyms are "dilemma," "plight," "perplexity," "bewilderment," and "doubt." None of these conveys the simple opposite of certainty, a condition marked not by puzzlement, anxiety, or frustration, but by confidence—even excitement—at the fact that we really don't know and, in the words of Richard Feynman, have before us "the pleasure of finding out." Thomas Henry Huxley's word "agnostic" will not do. It is still too colored by the denunciations of Huxley's opponents in the verbal battles of the late nineteenth century.

Whitehead's word was "muddle." It appears nowhere in his books that I know of, but any student of his will readily recall how often he used it in his classroom lectures. It was his way of describing where most of us are—himself included—most of the time. Those who think of themselves as being in a muddle, he used to say, have a far better chance of moving toward truth than those who think they have achieved it, whether in religion, philosophy, or anything else. There was nothing of perplexity, bewilderment, plight, or anxious doubting in the muddle Whitehead was talking about. It was instead an open candid acceptance of the human situation.

If Thales of Miletus in the sixth century B.C.E. was right in thinking that what passed for knowledge in his day could be improved upon, the same holds for us today. If we will bend ourselves to the task, some among us will be able to improve upon what passes for knowledge in our time. The clear implication of this state of affairs is, however, a basic uncertainty in all things. If what any generation looks upon as "knowledge" can be improved, then it cannot be true knowledge. It is only the best understanding we have achieved, at that time, of what we suppose true knowledge to be.

In short, as we approach the twenty-first century, we find ourselves where Thales found himself 2,500 years ago. We would like to improve our understanding of the nature of things as it exists today. We may, like Thales, be able to do so dramatically, or, perhaps, not at all. In any case, like Thales, we end where we began. We end in uncertainty as to what ultimate Truth is. If we are able to improve upon the understanding achieved by generations earlier than ours, we can be sure the generations following ours will be able to improve upon the concepts of truth we have formulated. That means neither of us enjoyed real certainty. It means that neither enjoyed the possession of true knowledge. At best, each had a formulation of truth, better than that of an earlier time, perhaps, but inevitably inferior to some future, as yet unanticipated formulation. Always we are left with ultimate uncertainty. Accordingly, our goal is not ultimate Truth, which we cannot attain, but ever greater understanding, which we can.

There is nothing new in a religion that clearly and boldly faces up to this situation. It is where religion has always been whenever it confronted life as we experience it at firsthand. The quarrel of the inquiring mind with the ecclesiastical mind on this point is in the latter's position that our uncertainty in ultimate things was overcome at some time in the past, and that the Truth achieved at that time is available to us today through dogma believed by faith. The new paradigm for religion finds such a position too optimistic. On all the evidence we today are where we were at the dawn of human consciousness. We were then, and we are now unable to penetrate divine mystery in any ultimate sense. To be sure, we are steadily gaining in knowledge and understanding, but as we do, ultimate mystery does not diminish and become knowledge. In some strange manner, as our knowledge increases, so, too, does mystery. Both, at the same time, grow larger, deeper, and seemingly more impenetrable than ever.

Skepticism

A declaration of ultimate uncertainty might seem to mean a reassertion of the ancient philosophy of skepticism. Is that where the religion of the open mind and heart comes out? Striving to state the faith of the new paradigm for religion, do we find that we can't, or that it hasn't any? Many a critic would nod in agreement and reply, yes indeed; that is what we have been saying all along. Liberalism, thought through to its basic implications, turns out to be classical skepticism. The new paradigm for religion is not a new form of faith; it is the destroyer of all faith; it is a position of ultimate doubt.

Let us admit for the moment that this would seem to be the logical outcome of the argument, that protest though we may, the new paradigm for religion does indeed end in quandary, with all the undesirable meanings that word carries. It is true that when we begin asking questions about our religious faith there is no place to stop. Questioning is like quicksand. Each step takes us farther until, if we pursue the questioning process all the way to the end, nothing remains but doubt.

We saw in chapter 3 that far back in ancient times, when alert minds in Greece began asking questions about the nature of things, one Pyrrho of Elis went all the way. A penetrating and consistent thinker, he found that on entering the questioning process one question led to another until he questioned everything and believed nothing. Pyrrho is only a legendary figure, but the position he reached so long ago is still the place where we are bound to come out, once we have asked the first question. Once begun, there is no end to the questioning process. Always another question lies beyond the one you have just answered until you come at last to a question you cannot answer. In matters of ultimate Truth, we do not know, cannot know, and never will know. That is our human condition.

But does that really bring us to a position of ultimate despair? Earlier than Pyrrho by nearly two centuries, Parmenides of Elea in ancient Greece had said that we cannot rely on our senses. Modern science has demonstrated the validity of Parmenides' surmise. Heraclitus, his contemporary, had insisted on the permanence of change. We now know that what looks and feels like solid matter is really a mass of swirling atoms. The everlasting hills wear away. New mountain chains rise to take their place. It is the same with our understanding of the universe and our concepts of right and wrong. They, too, slowly rise and have their day only to wear away and be replaced by others, presumably, but not necessarily, better. And which of us, living out our lives as best we can, has not found that amid the precious permanent things in life it is the constant change in our circumstances and condition that is permanent? The only ultimate permanence we know is our understanding of certain basic principles, of which the fact of change is among the most basic.

Living with Ultimate Uncertainty

Can we live in a world where we are never sure we really know, a world where the one thing we really know is that we really don't possess final answers to our questions? Donald Campbell, past president of the American Psychological Association, reiterated the suggestion that we are like sailors mending a rotting ship at sea. We trust the ship as a whole while we replace, one at a time, single planks that are rotten.[12] Karl Popper has a similar analogy: comparing our total body of knowledge to a set of piles driven into a bottomless bog. The trip-hammer that drives in a new pile to replace an old and rotting one is supported while it does so by the other piles. Together they provide a foundation from which a rotting pile can be extracted and a new one driven in to take its place.

The critical mind invites us into a religion built upon the principle of uncertainty, not in the limited sense in which Heisenberg formulated it, but in the universal sense in which David Hume stated it in his *Treatise of Human Nature*, as we saw in chapter 3. Following the most scrupulous analysis of our human condition that it was possible for him to make, Hume concluded that the certainty the religions claim and for which science and philosophy strive is unattainable. On this basic point he has never been proven wrong. Nevertheless, a whole lot remains after we have tested and quested to the uttermost, much more than we at first thought possible. What remains is the working knowledge we have accumulated by which we live. What is new, Hume said, is our understanding of the uncertain nature of that knowledge.

When we understand that all knowledge is ultimately uncertain but that it is useable nevertheless, we are at ease. When we realize that the knowledge we have is steadily growing in scope and clarity we are no longer troubled. Rather, we find ourselves with the sense of confidence in living that the established religions say they offer but which, in fact, they cannot provide. The difference is seen when questions arise in either thought structure. The established religions meet the questioner with an invitation to faith. In the new paradigm for religion the questioner is met with an invitation to ask more questions, to push the questioning process always further, as far as questions can carry it. At the end of the process the inquirer is invited to return to the belief structure that critical minds have been building and living by at least since Thales' time. Millions upon millions are now doing so. Back in the twelfth century Peter Abelard wrote: "By doubting we are led to inquire and by inquiry we perceive truth." His words might well be the motto of the new paradigm for religion today.

Slowly, steadily, inexorably, the approach to human knowledge hit upon by Thales has been invading religion. No priesthood elaborates it, few bodies of believers promote it, few institutions nurture it. Yet, while traditional religion strives to protect and update ancient thought and practice, many of the people it would serve have found answers to their questions, not in the "certainties" of faith, but in testing and questing in religion, never resting in the process.

Most questioners are not skeptics in any sense of the word. They are not doubters; they are inquirers. They set out on their quest, not in doubt but in anticipation. They yearn to pierce a little more deeply into the *mysterium tremendum* we all see surrounding us on every side. They do not expect to cut through to the heart of it. To be able to go even a little way further into it is more than enough for them. The new paradigm for religion exhibits its greatest strength at the point where its opponents see it as collapsing in ruin. The questioning process that is followed all the way to the end, as far as it can be pushed, does not lead to doubt and despair; it leads to further exploration. And while the exploring takes place and new knowledge is added to the old, we live according to what we have, better off because we have it, and eager for more as it becomes available to us.

Doubt

In the new paradigm for religion, then, the question is not: Do we live in a cloud of unknowing? That is where we start. It is neither a belief nor an article of faith. Like our seemingly inescapable human fallibility, not knowing the ultimate basis of life and of the universe is our human condition.

Uncertainty means doubt to most religious people, and that doubt has long been the bane of mainline religion. Cast your eye over the "New Books" shelf in almost any theological library and you are likely to see a shiny new volume, the latest essay on how to deal with doubt. If we can judge by the vast literature the defenders of ancient faith have produced over the centuries, doubt has been one of the most persistent problems with which traditional religion has had to contend.

The reason for the great clerical concern with doubt is the difficulty lay people have always had trying to understand and believe clerical teachings. The theology they offer is mostly ancient, often archaic in character, and literally incredible to a reasonable mind. A common clerical response to complaints by lay persons on this issue is to urge the questioners to have faith, to believe by sheer force of will because they resolve to believe. Such believing is taught as the triumph of religion over secularism.

Often such teaching succeeds. Often, however, it does not. Increasingly in the twentieth century it has not. A. N. Wilson, the English novelist, in a 1985 book *How Can We Know?* put the question to himself. "How can we know the Christian Way is true?" he asks. The more he thought about it the more he realized that despite his many doubts, he believed the Christian religion to be inescapably and irresistably true. The writing of the book became for him a rediscovery of "the Way, the Truth, and the Life."

Wilson makes it clear that his discovery was personal. It was a discovery for *him*. In writing the book he found that *he* believed. Yet he confessed that in the end he still doubted. In the same paragraph in which he says he believes, he restates the doubts with which he began. "I do not think," he concludes "that we shall ever find the answer to the question in my title *How Can We Know?* on this side of the grave."[13] The attempt really to believe ancient Christian teachings was obviously as difficult for him as it was nearly 2,000 years ago for the man Mark's Gospel tells us about who cried: "Lord, I believe. Help Thou mine unbelief!"[14] In the end, doubt, not belief, prevailed.

A favorite caricature of those who follow the way of inquiry in religion depicts them as groping about in the dark, hopelessly lost, searching for truth they cannot find, reduced at the last to doubting all beliefs and ultimately to despair. Doubt, however, is not a problem for the people of the new paradigm for religion. They do not fear doubt. They fear the cessation of inquiry.

Notes

1. Quoted in *Scientific American* (April 1982): 10.
2. Raymond Smullyan, *Forever Undecided* (New York: Alfred Knopf, 1987).
3. Percy Bridgman, *The Way Things Are* (Cambridge, Mass.: Harvard University Press, 1959).

4. James B. Conant, *On Understanding Science* (New Haven, Conn.: Yale University Press, 1947), p. 37.

5. James B. Conant, *Science and Common Sense* (New Haven, Conn.: Yale University Press, 1951), p. 25.

6. J. Robert Oppenheimer, *Science and the Common Understanding* (New York: Simon and Schuster, 1954).

7. Jacob Bronowski, *A Sense of the Future* (Cambridge, Mass.: MIT Press, 1977), p. 211.

8. Donald Culross Peattie, *Flowering Earth* (Indiana University Press, 1991).

9. Howard E. Gruber, review of Loren Eiseley, *Darwin and the Mysterious Universe* in *New York Times Book Review,* 22 July 1979, p. 16.

10. Peter Gay, *Reading Freud: Explorations and Entertainments* (New Haven, Conn.: Yale University Press, 1991).

11. Lewis Thomas, "On the Uncertainty of Science," *Key Reporter* (Autumn 1980): 1.

12. Donald T. Campbell, "Descriptive Epistemology: Psychological, Social and Evolutionary" (William James Lecture no. 4, Harvard University, 1977), p. 95.

13. A. N. Wilson, *How Can We Know?* (New York: Atheneum, 1985).

14. Mark 9:24.

12

Belief, Faith, and Thought

In Part One we reviewed the development of the new paradigm for religion in the West. In Part Two we set out to state the credo of the new paradigm. Now, seven chapters later, we still have no statement. We have, however, a set of conditions any statement of belief must meet if it is to be valid and therefore persuasive. We have fully faced up to the fact that the kind of certainty traditional religion has offered is not to be had.

Apparently a major problem with declarations of faith in the older mode is a failure to see what such declarations involve. The problem is partly one of word meanings. What do words like "belief" and "faith" mean? It is important to know in order that writer and reader may understand each other.

In theology it is particularly so because of the practice among theologians of redefining words. To retain old theological terminology, since grown sacred, can be very useful, but it can also be very deceptive. When old and honored words are defined in a new way—God, sin, belief, and faith, for example—the reader is often woefully misled. An example is the redefining of the word "revelation" dealt with in chapter 8. Accordingly, a final preliminary step must be taken before we attempt to draft any declaration of faith. We have first to be as clear as possible as to what we mean by what we say. Specifically, we need to be clear as to what we mean by those two fundamental religious terms "belief" and "faith."

The Belief Chart

Creeds and other codifications of religious thought are statements of belief. In the religions of the West belief is basic. Judaism, Christianity, and Islam have always set the highest value on the need to believe and on the importance of those beliefs being right. They must be a part of the authoritative body of doctrine of the religion in question. In the Judeo-Christian tradition, the importance of believing, and of "right" belief held a central place from the outset. Because of the importance of "right" belief Protestantism divided and subdivided into innumerable sects.

Westerners unthinkingly carry a kind of belief chart in their minds according to which they classify themselves and all other religious people. The orthodox and the conservatives are those who hold strictly to ancient beliefs in both concept and language. Liberals are those who want to change (liberalize) ancient beliefs. Those who retain and use the largest part of ancient belief patterns, usually quite literally, are regarded as the most conservative or orthodox. Those who are the least literal in their interpretation of word meanings are looked upon as the most liberal or radical. Orthodox Jews, devout Roman Catholics, Lutherans, and fundamentalist evangelical Protestants, for example, are looked upon as conservative; Friends, Unitarian Universalists, Ethical Society members, and Humanists are placed at the other end of the Western belief chart.

Where does the new paradigm for religion fall on such a chart? It has no place there at all. It has no official theology by which its "liberalism" or "conservatism" can be measured. The articles of faith in the new paradigm, as we shall see in Part Three, do not concern belief in gods, devils, spirits, supernatural forces, the Holy, the Infinite, the Eternal, or the Almighty. They do not proclaim a belief in transcendence or imminence. Neither do they call for belief in creation or annihilation, or in the occurrence of events like the miraculous crossing of the Red Sea as if it had been dry land, the Virgin Birth, or the Resurrection.

As the people of the new paradigm for religion see the situation, "belief" for most of the people of most of the religions of the West means "dogma." Their "beliefs" are the official teachings of the religion they profess. The adherents of a religion may or may not really believe those dogmas in their hearts. Often they do not. That is why doubt is such a problem in traditional religion. It is why "unbeliever," "skeptic," and "agnostic" are terms of opprobrium for them. Persistent doubt undermines a religion based on belief in events and in physical and metaphysical structures.

Creeds

In Christianity creeds play a central role. They have from the beginning. Initially they were simple declarations of faith made by converts at baptism. It was no small matter to make such a declaration when Christians were persecuted for their faith. Over time these confessions became formalized as a result of constant repetition. Quite naturally these formalizations began to vary from one another as Christianity overspread the Roman Empire. Controversy as to which declaration was the more authentic followed, and the resulting theological battles were often intense. The major ones were resolved at the great ecumenical Council of Nicaea held in 325 C.E. where the Nicene Creed was hammered out and agreed upon. It remains official in Christianity to this day.

Theology, they say, is the writing out of the raw stuff of religious experience. It is an attempt to catch in language the visions of the prophet and the songs of the poet and seer. Codification, interpretation, explanation—all these come long after, when the half-hidden truths in the living religious experience of an earlier generation become more apparent. Creeds appear when the philosophers and the theologians attempt to systematize the accumulated inspirations and intuitions of an earlier day. Eventually the words become holy. Not merely the symbol of the faith of the worshipper, in a very real sense the creeds themselves become the faith.

Creeds are an attempt to fashion that upon which the soul may feed and by which the spirit may live. They are an effort to bring eternity into time, to lay hold of the infinite within the finite, to describe in human terms a God who is superhuman and who, for this reason, eternally eludes both thought and language. Such was the Deuteronomic Code in Israel. It was drawn up at the close of the great prophetic period and was an attempt to reduce the ideals of the prophets to concrete doctrines and rules of conduct. Such were the creeds of Christendom as well. As Eric Hoffer observed: "The conservatism of religion—its orthodoxy—is the inert coagulum of a once highly reactive sap."[1]

Theology reduced to writing, formalized as a creed, as in the Nicene Creed for Christians, or in a code of law as with the Jewish Torah, acquires a dual handicap. "Creeds are at once the outcome of speculation and efforts to curb speculation," Whitehead once remarked with characteristic perceptivity.[2] But the successful curbing of theological speculation leads to immobility and stultification. A creed may successfully end theological turmoil as it did at Nicaea, but it brings original thinking to an end as well, as it also did at Nicaea. Thereafter thinking is confined to explaining, elaborating, or interpreting what has already been established and formally agreed upon. Creeds bring questing and testing to an end.

Dogmas are the dry husks of forgotten theological arguments. Creeds, it is often said, are out of date by the time they are drawn up and agreed upon. "Every intellectual revolution which has ever stirred humanity into greatness has been a passionate protest against inert ideas," said Whitehead on another occasion.[3]

A second factor draws creeds into a debilitating stability. Because they are genuinely useful, they tend to continue long in use. Soon they grow precious. Whatever is sacred to an earlier generation bears a double sanctity. People honor ancient creeds for their intrinsic worth, but soon they are honored yet more because of the reverence in which earlier generations have held them. Thus in the passing of the years, through constant repetition, the very words of the creeds become sanctified above and beyond the ideas and aspirations they were once designed to express. As a result, creeds can become so sacred and by the same token so immobile that no one dares to lay a hand upon them for any purpose, no matter how noble it may be.

Faith

Traditional religion, of course, agrees that one's beliefs should be very carefully examined. Unless a belief is valid, it cannot and should not be believed. What then is the difference between the two approaches to the problem of belief? It is simple but profound, easy to state, but far more difficult to accept. In traditional religion, belief is faith. In the new paradigm for religion belief may be faith, but usually it is not.

How do the two differ? Until recently any attempt to distinguish between belief and faith would have ended in failure. A credo, literally "I believe," was both a statement of belief and a declaration of faith. "Faith" meant formal assent to the official dogmas of the church. But it also meant living belief, deeply held as a conviction of the heart. Trust was an essential ingredient in such belief, trust that the truth attained by faith was Truth indeed. It meant trust in a Person or Power regarded as Ultimate, who guarantees the truth of what was believed. In medieval times and for many people today, "faith" means trust in a human institution—the church—the authority of which guarantees the truth of the beliefs it teaches. "Faith" is a "good" word. People of faith are thought of as good people. To have faith is a good thing. To be faithful is praiseworthy.

These meanings of the word are today understood and agreed upon. A standard dictionary definition says "faith" means belief in, trust in, and loyalty to God. A second definition states that "faith" also may mean trust in that for which there is no proof. This is a definition many Christians would give, relying on the language of the Epistle to the Hebrews 11:1, that faith is "the assurance of things hoped for, the conviction of things not seen."

It is here that contemporary theology gets us into trouble, however. In the hands of contemporary writers the word "faith" *may* mean believing with heart and soul what cannot be proved, but it may not. Seeking to make traditional religion acceptable to the contemporary mind, many a theologian has stretched the older established meaning almost to the breaking point. Your faith is your "total world outlook," your "life philosophy," says one writer. Another defines faith as "a way of knowing." Yet another tells us faith is "a way of living." It is "commitment to a way of life." Still another argues that faith is "human involvement in the ultimate mystery that confronts us all."

The new paradigm for religion stands against any such redefining of old and familiar theological terms. Thinking of faith as a way of life rather than the acceptance of the Nicene Creed, let us say, may help those who candidly admit that they do not—cannot—believe all the articles in the creed. But such redefinitions do not help those who try to think their theological problems all the way through. The inquiring mind is stood on its head when told that the commonly accepted meaning of "faith" is in error, that the word really means "your total world outlook," or simply, "a way of living." Thoughtful people are not helped by such intellectual gymnastics. For them, the result is neither knowledge nor inspiration; it is confusion and frustration.

Reading these new definitions, open-minded people feel as their forebears felt when Anselm, back in medieval times, exclaimed: "I believe in order that I may understand!" To the ordinary mind, Anselm had things backwards. Most of us would say, "When I understand, then I believe, because then I know what I am believing." In the new paradigm for religion theological problems are not solved by shifting word meanings. In the new paradigm for religion "faith" is not taken to mean any of the many things contemporary theology has suggested. It means what most people think it means, "the assurance of things hoped for, the conviction of things not seen"; or "belief and trust in that for which there is no proof"; or simply "trust in a Person or Power."

Having Faith

For the open mind there is a further problem. Merely *having* faith seems to be enough for many contemporary writers. It is not enough for the inquiring mind, however. If someone is said to have faith, the question immediately rises—or it should—what is that person's faith *in*? Fanatics are people of vibrant, compelling faith. To have faith may be a good thing, but it may not be. "Faith" is not a transitive verb. Perhaps it should be, as "love" is. Love has an object. So does faith. If, when we speak of faith, the object of our faith were stated, much of the ambiguity in the meaning of the term might be overcome.

Here the powerful voice of Martin Marty, mainline church historian and commentator, comes to the aid of the religion of the open mind and heart. On numerous occasions he has hooted from the stage of theological debate people who call upon us to believe or to trust without saying what our belief or trust is to be in. Typical was an outburst in his regular column in the *Christian Century* in 1986 where Marty identifies the phrase, "At least they believe in *something*" as a syndrome. It is, he says, the reaction of "secular and faintheartedly liberal commentators" who identify spiritual machismo among absolutists of various sorts. He cites as examples their defense of the counter-culture of the 1960s, of the fundamentalists of the 1970s, and of the arch-conservatives in the Roman Curia in the 1980s. When these groups were criticized, Marty asserts, the commentators came to their defense with the cliché, "By God, at least they believe in *something*."4 Without necessarily taking Marty's theological position, the critical mind heartily applauds such an all-too-rare volley from the ranks of mainline religion, pointing to the danger of "having" faith without looking to see what that faith is in.

As we shall see in Part Three, the idea of faith is not rejected in the new paradigm for religion. Faith lies at the heart of every true religion. But the open mind most emphatically rejects the idea, so often advanced today, that *having* faith is important. Merely having faith may be a very great evil. As a colossal example we have ever before us the horrors of the Hitler regime in Germany and the false believing that went with it. A brief reminder of the Jonestown story may help to sharpen the point, because it is less well-known and because it is specifically religious.

Jim Jones, an ordained minister in the Disciples of Christ Church, began his religious work as an ordinary clergyman in Indianapolis, Indiana. He was highly regarded because his church was genuinely interracial, and because it in fact served the poor and dispossessed. When Jones established a new movement under his own personal leadership in Mendocino County, California, in 1964, he was already recognized as a powerful charismatic figure. Because of mounting criticism and rising suspicion that he was both fraudulent and dangerous, he later moved his "Peoples Temple" to Port Kaituma in Guyana. The mass murder and suicide of the entire group that followed left the world numb with disbelief and horror.

Whoever would question the central principle of the new paradigm for religion—the need for testing to the uttermost what we believe to be true—must deal with Nazism, Jonestown, and the principle of dictatorship itself. The first thing any dictator suppresses is the freedom to question the policies, programs, statements, or actions of the governing body. Checking and testing—criticism—is the one thing dictatorships cannot endure.

Exposing flaws destroys dictatorships as the sun melts the snow in the spring. Inquiry destroys the illusion of omniscience on which dictatorships are built, gain acceptance, and establish authority. Exposure destroys the falsehoods on which dictatorships rest. For this reason the practice of testing for truth, testing to the uttermost, has become the cornerstone of the thought structure of the West. Where we are failing today, there are the areas where truth is hidden. Where questioning is forbidden, where testing does not occur, there falsehood, deceit, and perversion flourish.

Our task, the Enlightenment people say, is to see that error, deceit, and fraud are always with us, even in religion. Human deceit and human error know no limitations. Neither sanctity nor holiness nor divinity are protection against them. Our assignment as human beings of limited capacity is not to weep or to rail at our condition. Rather, in the new paradigm for religion, alert in mind and cheerful in heart, we are required to expect human error and search it out; to expect deceit and eliminate it. It is our task to eliminate them and move on toward truth and right in religion, as we do in everything else.

Formulation

In the new paradigm for religion, belief and faith turn out to be very simple. Both are readily achieved by anyone. They do not require skilled theologians. They are simply the best statement we can make at any given time and in any given place of what we conceive the truth to be about whatever matter is before us.

Such a statement can be very simple. It can be very elaborate. Crucial, however, is that we understand what a belief is, how it is held, and what it does. In the new paradigm for religion a belief is a thought. It is an idea. It is a concept we have formulated. It is not carved in stone or set in concrete. The beliefs of an inquirer are held openly. They are ever ready to be clarified, expanded, deepened, or dropped if found fatally erroneous. Such a belief is really believed, but as a formulation only.

The religion of the open mind and heart does not reject as false the tenets of other religious faiths. We must distinguish rejection from nonacceptance. What the critical mind rejects is the idea that beliefs in religion can be handed down to us from the skies and canonized within a church. In the eyes of the inquirer religious beliefs are slowly evolved through human effort here on earth. The result is not looked upon as absolute truth we would not otherwise possess. It is seen as neither final nor unchangeable. Such truth as we humans know is the best formulation we are able to draw up of what we believe the truth to be at any given time in any given place.

In the new paradigm for religion, then, the first concern is not to draw up a declaration of faith. The first question is not: What do we believe? In the religion of the open mind and heart there is no Apostles' Creed, no Nicene Creed, no Thirty-nine Articles, no Statement of Faith, no Torah or other Scriptures declared to be sacred. There is instead a commitment to openness in the formulation of whatever beliefs we hold. That commitment is total. No subject is too sacred to be explored. No pronouncement is too sacrosanct to be tested, and no person is too holy to be questioned. For the open mind and heart it is the truth that is holy.

In the clamor of conflicting beliefs among the religions of earth, what do we hear in the new paradigm for religion? We hear not a declaration or a proclamation, but an invitation. And it is not an invitation to accept yet another set of beliefs. It is an invitation to all of us to examine and ponder the beliefs of all the religions including those of the new paradigm. It is not an invitation to have faith. It is an invitation to consider the articles of faith that others have and to see what validity there may be in them.

Inquirers think of their beliefs not as Truth descended from heaven, but as formulations of truth fashioned here on earth. In the new paradigm our beliefs are the most accurate and the most adequate formulations we can contrive of what we think the truth is. No aspect of truth is more certain than that eventually someone will be able to state it more accurately and more adequately than we have. Inquirers believe all of this with heart and soul and mind and strength. They believe that the belief structures they devise provide useful workable thought patterns for living. This is their faith. They are always ready to test it by whatever means can be devised, and to restate it if a better formulation can be found.

The End of Contention

Once it is understood that articles in a creed are neither statements of fact nor declarations of eternal Truth, but formulations of what we think the facts are and of what we think the Truth might be— once that is understood, a remarkable change takes place in us. We are no longer in contention with one another. We no longer think that those who disagree with us are tragically mistaken or a threat to the rest of us. We no longer feel the need to try to convert them to our set of beliefs.

The basic difference between religion in the old paradigm and in the new is not that they hold conflicting beliefs. The difference is in the attitude each takes toward the believing process. The beliefs that are to be found in the new paradigm for religion often do not differ from those we find in traditional religion. But they differ profoundly in the manner in which the beliefs are held. For the inquirer, believing is an open-ended process. In the new paradigm for religion, any part of any belief structure is open to additions, deletions, or modifications of any kind at any time.

We have been accustomed to think of rivalry and contention between the religions and between factions within the religions as primarily doctrinal in character. In fact, most of them are. But doctrinal differences are of little concern to inquiring minds. For them the main difference is not doctrine; it is attitude. Our task, say the inquirers, is to take a new look at the believing process. We have now to see that in religion our beliefs must have the same standard of acceptance and rejection they have in every other field of human endeavor. We have now to see that the solution to the problem of conflicting beliefs does not consist in finding the best doctrines and dogmas. It consists in a new understanding of what doctrines, dogmas, and beliefs are.

A credo drawn up in accordance with the standards we have formulated in the preceding chapters would not be like the Nicene Creed, a set of articles beginning "I believe in one God. . . ." It would begin, "I believe religious beliefs are formulations only. They are not statements of Eternal Truth. They are the best formulations we have been able to make, stating our best understanding of the nature of things." These articles of faith gain no special privileges in the hall of truth when they are held by a church or temple, a cult or tradition thought by its devotees to have been divine in origin. In the new paradigm for religion all of the articles of faith of all the religions stand alike before the bar of human judgment. Any authority they possess is internal, not external. None gains ascendancy over the others through self-asserted authority, holiness, or sanctity.

It is the validity of a belief that is paramount. Neither passionate believing, nor towering faith can change that one single overarching fact: validity comes first. How we establish the validity of our articles of faith thereby becomes a matter of the first importance. How that is done distinguishes the new paradigm for religion, not the particular beliefs it holds. Clear, stern, hard thinking as to what beliefs it should hold marks the religion of the open mind and heart. The Western intellectual tradition, the university tradition in religion, the new paradigm for religion—whatever name we may give it—is distinguished by its commitment to the truth-seeking process. When that commitment is total, the open heart and mind and spirit are confident that any resulting articles of faith will turn out to be all that we might desire.

Notes

1. Eric Hoffer, *The True Believer* (New York: Harper & Brothers, 1951), p. 3.

2. A. N. Whitehead, *Adventures of Ideas* (New York: Macmillan Co., 1905), p. 66.

3. A. N. Whitehead, *The Aims of Education* (New York: The Macmillan Co., 1929), p. 2.

4. Martin Marty, "M.E.M.O.," *Christian Century* (November 26, 1986): 1079.

Part Three

Four Articles of Faith

An unrelenting attempt to state in positive terms the Liberal Protestant Christian faith does not end where it is expected to, with a set of beliefs. It ends with a set of standards any declaration of faith must meet if it is to state what the believers really believe.

A set of articles prescribed by an organized religion is something quite different. There the adherents give assent to, and they endeavor to believe, an officially established creed. Its several articles may or may not be genuine beliefs. They may or may not tell the worshippers what the meaning of life is for them. Such "beliefs" are options at best that are accepted or rejected according to the appeal they have for the faithful. At worst they are empty words.

On the other hand, an attempt to state beliefs we really believe ends, not with a creed, but with conditions for creed-making. A quick check of the topics that emerged in Part Two shows this very clearly. First, if our beliefs are to be genuine, if we are to hold them deep down inside, so that we live by them, we must believe beyond doubting that they are true. We must believe they are as valid as we can make them, and as accurate as our fallible human faculties will permit. In short, they must have been thoroughly tested for validity. Second, if our beliefs are really to guide our thoughts and actions, we must also believe that they have been pushed to the outer limits of our human comprehension and to the outer limits of our imagination as well. Our questing, like our testing, must have been total. Third, never resting in the process must have been our will and way.

Fourth, beyond all that, we must believe that no unacknowledged exceptions have crept in—exceptions that would, by their presence, undercut the beliefs we have already stated. Fifth, we must believe yet further that our beliefs have been arrived at after a full, open, and free exchange at all levels as to their validity. Beliefs tested in this exacting manner are truly believed. They are not threatened by questioning. Testing confirms them. Open debate does not jeopardize true beliefs, it strengthens them. Such beliefs are not believed by an act of will. Sixth, our beliefs must be ours, even after a thorough-going comparison with the beliefs that have developed in religions other than our own. Where the foregoing conditions have been met, our beliefs have become so persuasive they compel believing, sometimes almost against our will.

Even then, in the end we are forced to concede that we live in "a cloud of unknowing." Uncertainty is our human lot when we come to ultimates. We do not say that this is how things must be—only that this is the way things are. It is what we find when we look at our beliefs. No belief is more securely grounded than that of our ultimate uncertainty with regard to all of them.

Does that leave us bereft as so many traditionalists suppose? No, and for two very good reasons: (1) Religion in the old paradigm cannot take us from uncertainty to certainty any better than religion in the new paradigm can. The ardor of traditional faith does not make the object of that faith either more real or more certain. Passionate belief may be compelling for those who hold it, but for those who do not it is a source of amazement, not of persuasion. (2) In place of the conflicting claims and the turmoil passionate believing brings about, the new paradigm for religion offers principles and concepts. These are not revelations from on high. They are ideas formulated by searching and exploring, confirmed by open inquiry and debate. We humans can live by concepts as successfully as ever we lived by the dogmas of traditional faith. We can do it better. Concepts have an enormous advantage over dogmas. They can tolerate one another's presence and they have the capacity for growth even while we are living in accordance with them.

With the foregoing conditions clearly before us, let us see whether we can formulate a statement of faith that will meet the demands they place upon us. The four articles that follow have not been developed in an ecclesiastical council, the usual practice in traditional religion. They are not derived from the sacred scriptures of an estab-lished religion. They are not derived from alleged divine revelations, either ancient or modern. They are derived from the thought of the ages, both sacred and secular. They are among the most basic beliefs we humans have been able to formulate. We accept them and make them ours because we are unable to *dis*believe them. They are the bedrock upon which a belief structure that meets the foregoing conditions stands.

13

Bedrock

When you dig down through the soil in New England, you first strike humus, then sand, and finally hardpan. Beneath that, particularly in the uplands, you come to bedrock, often sooner than you expect. That means you have come to a ledge, a part of the basic contour of the landscape. You have come to Earth's mantle itself. You are on bedrock and can go no farther—at least not without a power drill or dynamite.

Bedrock in religion, as in nature, is where you come to rest because, for all practical purposes, you can go no further. In New England's hill country, bedrock is usually granite. In traditional religion the ultimate final concept is God. "To believe in the Universe is to believe in God, and to believe in God is to believe in the Universe," it is often said. A statement like that means everything, which is also to say it means nothing. Nevertheless, it is typical of the end result of many a traditional attempt to get back to the basics of belief. What do we get back to when we dig down to the basics in the new paradigm for religion? What is the solid rock upon which its foundation rests?

The present inquiry illustrates the point. We have been working backward from the disorganized mass of experience with which life confronts us, to a statement of the principles or concepts on which it all rests, principles so basic that they themselves rest on nothing but their own validity. Basic principles or articles of faith of this character are not laid down at the outset of an inquiry like this one; they are disclosed at the end of it. But if we are delineating the process by which we are trying to make sense out of the chaos of human experience, our basic principles are stated at the beginning.

We start from them. They are the foundation upon which the system of thought we are building rests. Basic principles are the beginning and the end of the thinking process, both at the same time. Which way we say it depends on what we are trying to say.

Basic principles are not believed by an exercise of the will to believe. They are not believed because some authority has declared that they are true. They are believed because nothing can be formulated in the area they cover that seems to us to be more basic and therefore nearer to the truth. If a more fundamental statement could be made, we would make it. That statement would then replace the one we had previously made. Out of its own inner validity a new statement would replace a predecessor that was seen to be inferior. We do not choose our basics, they choose us. They are ours because we cannot think of anything more basic. An open mind is driven to them. They are beliefs that compel believing.

In religion, where we deal with the basics of life, we cannot pick and choose ideas that happen to suit our taste. In any true belief pattern we believe what we must. We believe what seems to us to be unavoidably, inescapably true. If, for example, we say we believe God will protect us from our enemies, but we build aircraft carriers, tanks, flying fortresses, nuclear weapons, and project a star wars program, it is clear that, whatever our theology may be, we have been driven to the conclusion that in war we rely not on God, but on the machinery of war we ourselves have built.

In cosmology we have been driven to believe in the Big Bang because no other concept so well explains all the phenomena the cosmologists have recently been discovering. For inquirers basic questions must be answered with more than a rejoinder. Our answers to basic questions must possess us. Our response to the teachings of our religion must be "Yes! That's it! Now I understand. Now I believe." When we can exclaim spontaneously "Yes! That's it!" we have true belief. That means we have faith. That means that we believe, even though we cannot prove, the truth of what we are saying.

Self-Evident Truth

The Founding Fathers of the United States, struggling with this question while drafting the Declaration of Independence, used the phrase "self-evident truth." It was not their invention. They found it in John Locke's *Essay Concerning Human Understanding*. In fact, "self-evident truth" is not Jefferson's language as we usually suppose. His intention, he said, had been "to place before mankind the common sense of the subject." Benjamin Franklin, it is now believed, suggested the phrase "self-evident" for the Declaration of Independence.

The concept goes all the way back to classical times, when the idea of Natural Law was formulated. We can trace it as far back as Plato and Aristotle. A clear statement of the concept was made by the Roman Stoics, Cicero in particular. He held that human laws, when they are right and just, embody a natural law that we humans can discover and state. Natural Law is a part of the structure of the universe. As such, it stands beyond the best of our human formulations.

Traditional religion tends to look on the idea of self-evident truth with disdain because there is no agreement among philosophers as to what truths *are* self-evident. Some philosophers dismiss the idea altogether on the ground that it is in itself invalid. Critical minds would reply that the seemingly self-evident character of a particular truth does not prove its validity. It is, however, an indication that we are in the presence of a declaration as basic as any that can be made. A self-evident truth is simply that: a statement of something that seems to be so true that few if any can reasonably deny it; which is another way of saying it is genuinely believed to be true. People act as if it were true, which is yet another way of saying it is deeply believed. Self-evident truths are beliefs that compel believing because it makes no sense to doubt them.

The concept of self-evident truth is a dual one; it is both static and dynamic. It is static in the sense that it requires a flat statement, as when our forefathers asserted that all men are endowed with certain inalienable rights. It is dynamic in the sense that statements of it are subject to change. As an example, not only all *men*, but all *people* are endowed with certain inalienable rights—women as well as men. The self-evidence in a truth has constantly to demonstrate itself. A supposed truth remains self-evident only as long as it cannot successfully be improved upon. The Founding Fathers did not stop to ponder what it meant to speak of self-evident truth. To them the fact that truth is self-evident was itself self-evident.

Unless a religion has been tested for validity to the uttermost, its sacredness, beauty, ancient and hallowed origins, the depth and scope of its theology will not mean very much. Because we live by our religion, it must have at its heart a self-evident, self-persuading character. To be like a painting hanging on the wall, good to look at, interesting to study, beautiful perhaps, but something we can take or leave—for theology that is not enough. If our religion is to direct our lives as we expect it to do, it must *possess* us. We cannot take it or leave it, according to our personal preference or whim or taste, and we cannot be plagued with doubts about its validity.

Truth, when it is self-evident, lays hold of us like the sunset glow at twilight. We don't argue about the beauty of such a scene. It speaks directly to us. So with basic principles. They bear within themselves the power to persuade. They leave us without the power of denial. Truth, validity, once beheld, remains. Only something that seems to be yet more valid or true can dislodge it. Critically minded people seek beliefs that have such a self-commendatory character, like believing in the ocean tide or the succession of day and night. Inquirers do not think of truth as a dove that descends to us from heaven, full grown and beautiful. For them truth is like a flower that slowly unfolds in the warmth and light of the sun.

What Is Truth?

Are we merely playing word games here? If we say that basic principles or concepts are formulations not of total, absolute, final Truth, but of what we think the truth is, what have we said? What is truth? To answer that question we have definitions enough. A standard *Dictionary of Philosophy and Religion* lists five:

1. The correspondence theory (the "true" corresponds to reality, which comes closest to the common understanding of the term most of us have).

2. The coherence theory (the "true" is the coherent system of ideas).

3. The pragmatic theory (the "true" is the "workable" or satisfactory solution of a problematic situation).

4. The semantic theory (assertions about truth are in a metalanguage and apply to statements of the base language).

5. The performative theory (the assertion that truth is the performative act of agreeing with a given statement).[1]

Sorting out and trying to grasp the difference among these five concepts of truth does not help the average person very much. For our purposes the *Merriam Webster* is better. Seeking the common understanding of what the term conveys to the average person, this reference defines truth as fact, actuality, or transcendent reality, often capitalized; or as the quality of keeping close to fact by avoiding distortion and/or misrepresentation.[2] At the philosophical level Whitehead is more helpful. In his *Adventures of Ideas* he wrote: "Truth is a qualification which applies to appearance alone. Reality is just itself and it is nonsense to ask whether it be true or false. Truth is the conformation of Appearance to Reality. . . . Truth is a generic quality with a variety of degrees and modes."[3]

Earlier in his *Religion in the Making*, Whitehead had remarked: "Progress in truth—the truth of science and the truth of religion—is mainly a progress in the framing of concepts."[4] James Bryant Conant, describing the purpose and meaning of science, used almost the same language. In general agreement with the foregoing, Jacob Bronowski once observed that a statement is true when it corresponds to the facts. He conceded that "facts" are not easy to come by. You determine what they are first by close observation, then by checking and rechecking. Next you conceptualize. That means you relate the facts you already have to the facts you are in the process of identifying. You then relate them all to one another within a single conceptual scheme.[5]

The result of this process is a constant overthrow of both the facts and the conceptual schemes you already have, and their replacement by still better ones. Bronowski's emphasis is not only on the checking and correcting process. It is also on the constant development of new conceptual schemes that will better unify and connect previously unrelated data, the process we dealt with in chapter 6 on questing. "There is an essential coarseness in the world," Bronowski wrote on another occasion, and added: "this coarseness is the real meaning of Heisenberg's principle of uncertainty."[6] No one has stated the idea of truth as it has emerged in the Western intellectual tradition more succinctly.

The critical mind does not ask: What is truth? It asks: How can we best formulate what we believe the truth to be? The question is not: Which of several doctrines is the more sound? It is: How best can we formulate sound doctrine? As in philosophy and science, so in the new paradigm for religion, we begin with the universe that surrounds us. We have nowhere else to begin if our minds and hearts are open—if we have not decided in advance what the answer to our question is to be. That means we begin with all the data of experience and with all the accumulated knowledge of the ages as well. It means that we begin with all the traditions and teachings, decrees, dogmas, and sacred scriptures of all the religions also. From that incredibly large and complex mass of data, in the new paradigm for religion we move toward a formulation of what the truth might be like if we were able to state in language what it is.

The inquirer is not dedicated to particular formulations of truth that have already been drawn up. Herein lies the uniqueness of the new paradigm for religion. The inquirer is dedicated to drawing up the best formulation of truth we can achieve in the present, including and checked against the noblest and most sacred formulations drawn up in the past. The inquirer does not neglect any of the theological formulations that have already been made. All are carefully weighed and assessed for their spiritual quality, but also for their validity. Those that are noble and persuasive are kept. Those that are ignoble or partly persuasive or both are used to the fullest extent possible, not forgetting that. They are used as formulations only, to be improved, modified, or given up entirely whenever better ones are found.

At this point we find ourselves asking once again: Are we not lost in words here, saying nothing really in an attempt to solve an unsolvable problem? Such a danger surely besets an inquiry like this. Going back then to bedrock, let us for the purposes of the present inquiry agree on the commonly accepted meaning of "truth." Let us lay aside subtle philosophies, theologies, etymologies, and linguistic refinements. By "truth" let us mean what a standard dictionary says most people understand the word to mean: freedom from falsity and error, and a correspondence of what we are saying to what is; that is to say a correspondence to Reality, insofar as that goal is achievable.

The concept of truth in the new paradigm for religion is Greek. It is the concept of truth on which the culture of the West is built. Although rejected in the Christian West in the early centuries of our era, the ancient Greek concept of truth never died out. The evidence that observation and reflection presented to alert Western minds constantly raised doubts about Christian insistence that Truth in fundamental matters was already in hand. Gradually, the Greek view reasserted itself in Western culture until today, except in Western religious thought, it is almost universally accepted.

Traditional religion seems not to see where the contemporary Western mind is today. The Western mind is not Judaic or Christian, as we commonly suppose, and it is not Islamic. It is Greek, and as much by use as by inheritance. The Western mind-set is Greek because Greek concepts put to use in the Western world as a whole provided a thought structure that made for the extraordinary advances in human achievement and understanding our planet has witnessed, especially in recent centuries. The Greek idea of looking at what we see around us, of studying and collating the data of experience, yielded the astonishing results of which we today are the beneficiaries. These in turn suggested and then produced yet sharper observations, and yet broader, deeper, and more exact concepts through which to grasp the meaning of those observations. The first dramatic result of this attitude was the university tradition as it developed early in the Middle Ages and eventually became the Western intellectual tradition as we see it in full flower today.

Truth in Traditional Religion

For the defenders of ancient faith, however, truth is not something that lies at the end of a long process of testing and questing. In traditional religion truth in fundamental matters is not sought; it is already in hand. Its source and authority is an ancient revelation believed to have been divine. An oft-quoted line from John's Gospel illustrates the point. It reads: "Ye shall know the truth and the truth shall make you free."[7] Few Bible passages are quoted more often, and fewer are more often misinterpreted. These words are almost always cited in support of the ideal of truth-seeking, one of the most basic ideals of the Western intellectual tradition. Nearly all of those who quote them believe these words are a promise that we humans shall know the truth one day, and that when we do freedom will be our reward.

Yet a quick reference to the Bible will show that that is far from what the words mean in context. In the previous verse John makes his meaning abundantly clear. The full passage reads: "Jesus then said to the Jews who had believed in him, 'If you continue in my word, you are truly my disciples, and you will know the truth and the truth will make you free.' "[8] The truth that makes us free, according to the full text, is not truth taken as a whole. Truth, in this passage is the belief that Jesus was the Messiah whose coming had been predicted in ancient Jewish literature, our present Old Testament. For many Christians, that is indeed a statement of ultimate, final Truth. For many other Christians, however, it is not, nor is it a statement of the truth for Jews or for other non-Christians.

Karl Barth, who polarized Protestant Christian thought in the twentieth century, held stoutly to the doctrine of truth stated in John's Gospel. Summarizing his views in the early 1960s, Barth wrote: "The positive factor [in my point of view] was this . . . Christian doctrine, if it is . . . to build up the Christian Church . . . has to be exclusively and conclusively the doctrine of Jesus Christ as the Living Word of God spoken to us men."[9] He may or may not be right, but for us that is not what is significant in his statement. Conspicuous in it is the lack of any reference to the truth of the doctrine on which he would build his church.

Though a doctrine may build ten thousand churches, it is nothing for the inquirer, unless truth be the foundation upon which it stands. Ramses II, Pharaoh of Egypt, was the greatest temple builder who ever lived, if the number of temples and the weight of the stone in them is our measure. But are we persuaded of the truth of Egyptian religion in the second millennium B.C.E. by the massive remains of Ramses' building program? Do they help us to believe that the chief god to whom those temples were reared, Amon Re, ever existed? Does the immenseness of Ramses' effort say anything about the truth of his religion? Karl Barth, of course, was thinking of church-building in a far deeper sense than the constructing of massive stone monuments. But the question for inquirers is the same in both instances. Unless truth lies at the heart of a religion, what matters that it be large or strong in any other respect?

For the inquirer it is irrelevant to point out that a particular doctrine will build up the church. That is surely a desirable goal, but no church, no temple, no religion, no system of churches can be an end in itself. For the inquirer the real question is the validity of what the church or religion is teaching. Whether a doctrine fills or empties a church is not the question. The benefits that result from a doctrine are of importance, to be sure, but they are not the measure of its validity or its worth. In the short run the benefits may seem to be a valid measure. But in the long run, in the light of our knowledge of our capacity to err, the only doctrine that will build a church that will meet our religious needs is one that has been tested for truth until no more tests can be devised by which to determine how much truth there is in it, and until it has been expanded to the outermost limits a soaring mind and spirit can attain.

Truth, Goodness, and Beauty

The differences between religion in the new paradigm and traditional religion should not obscure from us the many beliefs and practices the two paradigms hold in common. The devotion of both to the ideals of love and justice, goodness and mercy is the same. For this reason, in stating the beliefs of the new paradigm for religion, there is little stress on matters of virtue. Both traditions insist upon intense, thorough-going, total loyalty to the virtues, few if any of which could be called exclusively or even primarily Christian or Jewish, Islamic or Buddhist, or "secular."

It is on the issue of truth that the two paradigms divide, and that is why so much of the writing by inquirers is devoted to this issue. Inquiry in religion usually results in a protest movement. The questioner asks for much closer attention to the truth of religious teachings than traditional religion has given. Inquiry centers in the idea of truth because, as we saw in chapter 8, traditional religion does not accept the truth-seeking process of the Western mind *in religion*. The inquiring mind does not value dogma; it values the truth that dogma tries to state. Inquirers flatly reject the demand of religious leaders that they be granted special privileges in the court of truth. For the inquirer truth is sacred in its own right. It does not become more sacred when it is "religious." Nor does truth become any truer when committed to the custody of the saints. In fact, on the record that history gives us, truth in the hands of the holy is at grave risk.

To conclude, truth is not the only concern in the new paradigm for religion. The ancient Greek mind at its apex developed the complex and highly integrated triune concept of truth, goodness, and beauty. Of the three, Western religion—specifically Judaism, Christianity, and Islam—centers upon goodness with some attention to beauty, but none at all on truth, at least not as the Greeks understood the term. All three religions speak much of truth, to be sure, but for them the truth is the special teachings of their own particular brand of religion. Where the Greeks sought fervently to learn what the truth was, Judaism, Christianity, and Islam declare themselves already to be in possession of it. God has revealed it to them, they say. The world has only to accept it, believe it, interpret it, and persuade all others to do the same.

The Greeks taught us that truth is like beauty and goodness. It is not something inherited from ancient times that we now possess. Neither is it something a benign deity has conferred upon us. Truth is a vision that lies before us. Like beauty, goodness, and love, truth is a goal that is still to be achieved. For the Greek mind truth, in religion and in all things, is like beauty and goodness. It is something we now know only in part. With all three—truth, goodness, and beauty—that which is perfect is still to come.

In our attempt to understand all three, we know that our human shortcomings limit us greatly. Our frailty besets us quite as much when we seek truth as it does when we are in pursuit of beauty and goodness. In all three avarice and greed distort our vision, but hope and aspiration, insight and vision lead us on, even while we know that total and complete truth, beauty, and goodness may never be ours.

Notes

1. William L. Reese, *Dictionary of Philosophy and Religion: Eastern and Western Thought* (New Jersey: Humanities Press, 1980), p. 588.

2. *Merriam Webster's Ninth New Collegiate Dictionary.*

3. A. N. Whitehead, *Adventures of Ideas* (New York: Macmillan Co., 1935), p. 309.

4. A. N. Whitehead, *Religion in the Making* (New York: Macmillan Co., 1926), p. 131.

5. Jacob Bronowski, *A Sense of the Future* (Cambridge, Mass.: MIT Press, 1977), p. 230.

6. Ibid., p. 230.

7. John 8:32.

8. John 8:31-32.

9. Karl Barth, "How My Mind Has Changed in the Decade: Part Two," *Christian Century*, Centennial Issue (July 4-11, 1985): 684.

14

The Self

Setting out to state some of our most basic beliefs according to the standards of the new paradigm for religion, we begin with the self. In the new paradigm for religion René Descartes was right. We begin in the here and now. We begin with the individual, with the self that each of us is. In stating what we can be sure of, we begin with you and me.

We do not do this because we have adopted Cartesian philosophy as our own. We begin where we are, as we are, for the same reason Descartes did—because we have no other choice. Here is where we are, wherever "here" is. "Now" is when we are here, whenever "now" is, and knowledge and understanding is what we make of the experience that is ours where we are at the present moment.

Belief in the Self

The inquirer holds that our questions will be answered here on earth, if they are answered at all, not in the hereafter, about which we know nothing. They will be answered by people like you and me, at work on the problem, not by voices from the sky speaking some angelic language, or by religious officials precipitating the confusion, argument, and strife the religions have known down the ages.

The inquirer holds also that our true beliefs come to us directly, not at second hand. They are not reported to us by saint, seer, prophet, mystic, or Sacred Personage to be accepted as delivered from on high. Our true beliefs are not believed on the authority of a church, a religious tradition, or an official of some sort. Although we may be quite wrong in interpreting the meaning of our experiences, at least the interpretations are ours. When we rely on personal firsthand experience and our own understanding of it, we do not have to wonder, as we must, even with Holy Writ, whether or not the report and/or the transcript we are getting from someone else is accurate.

When we rely upon ourselves we do not do so because we think the self is the most reliable or the most important thing in the universe. We do so because, insofar as we know anything, we know that each of us as an individual exists. It is we, each of us, who face these dilemmas. It is we who ask the questions. It is we who seek the best answers we can find to the questions. It is we who have to choose among the various answers that are before us, and it is we who have experiences the meaning of which we are trying to understand.

To believe in the self is to see the self as a separate entity. And what is that? Marvin Minsky, a leading authority on artificial intelligence, writes: "Self is the part of mind that's really me, or rather it's the part of me—that is, part of my mind—that actually does the thinking and wanting and deciding and enjoying and suffering. It's the part that's most important to me because it's that which stays the same through all experience—the *identity* which ties everything together."[1]

Susan Krieger, social critic, advocates an inner individual view of the self, and argues for the importance of taking that point of view in social studies. "I do not think that the more full development of individual and inner perspectives will result in the downfall of social science," she writes, "nor will it lessen our abilities to understand the world outside ourselves. Rather . . . I believe that increased personal understanding can help us think more intelligently and fully about social life."[2] Her belief in the centrality of self comes out of her own personal experience. "In recent years," she continues, "I have increasingly come to think in personal terms about the social science I do."[3]

To believe in the self means having faith in the capacities the self finds in itself to think. It is neither a dream nor an illusion, but more or less all that it seems to us to be. Going further, it means believing that we humans can succeed in the tasks we have set for ourselves, even if only in part. Through a religion that is open, each of us can grow in knowledge and understanding. We can begin to grasp the meaning of life. We can make life a little better. To succeed we must look to the present and the future as well as to the past. We must test our judgments, not against ancient dogma, but against our clearest thinking in the present, against our broadest and most profound experiences in the present, and against the experience and judgment of those around us.

The classical statement of this point of view is Ralph Waldo Emerson's essay "Self Reliance." He writes: "Speak your latent conviction and it shall be the universal sense. . . . The highest merit we ascribe to Moses, Plato, and Milton is that they set at naught books and traditions, and spoke not what people but what they [themselves] thought. We should learn to detect and watch that gleam of light which flashes across the mind from within more than the luster of the firmament of bards and sages. . . . Trust thyself," he continues. "Every heart vibrates to that iron string. . . . The great person is the one who in the midst of the crowd keeps with perfect sweetness the independence of solitude."[4]

No Hubris

Utterances like these resulted in the denunciation of the Liberals by the traditionalists. The Liberals were too optimistic and too self-assured, it was said. To be sure, for some Liberals the idea of progress onward and upward forever became a dogma. Beginning with the self as the Liberals do admittedly sounds egocentric, self-satisfied, and self-important. The Liberals were a classic example of *hubris*, the traditionalists said. Arrogance, the sin of pride, of which traditional religion has made much over the years, foreordained their own downfall, the traditionalists said.

Closer examination, however, shows that the traditional, not the Liberal, attitude is the one of pride, while that of the inquirer is one of genuine humility. The starting point of the traditionalists in religion is that of a Deity who created and rules the universe, who placed humanity at the center of it, and made us his/her central concern. We humans are the crowning achievement of such an all-powerful, yet loving Creator, the traditionalists say. He/she holds us in her/his attentive, solicitous care.

To the inquirer that doctrine is a supreme example of the sin of self-importance, the ultimate among the sins of pride which are anathema in traditional religion. The new paradigm for religion holds a much more modest view of the human creature's place in the cosmos. For the inquirer the studies of the anthropologists, biologists, geologists, and evolutionists during the last several centuries make it very clear that we humans are creatures of earth like the worms and spiders, clams and dinosaurs, tigers, baboons and chimpanzees. Our record in the history books shows us to be fallible in the extreme. We are not merely error-prone. Too often we are deceitful, vicious, and of decidedly evil intent. We slaughter one another in war and today we are despoiling this planet, our home, while we overpopulate it and think of shipping our waste to the moon before we are inundated by it.

Is this the creature whom God made a little lower than the angels and covered with glory and honor, the inquirer asks? Looking at the realities in the case—all of them—the people in the Western intellectual tradition call for a review of the argument. On the *hubris* issue—that of self-importance, exaggerated pride in the self—they think the traditionalists might well reexamine their own position and ask: Are we humans really God's supreme creation?

Let us be clear that the confidence of the inquirer in the self is not based on what we humans have done, even the best of us. Nor is it based on what we are now doing. In the new paradigm for religion, our faith lies not in what we are, but in what we have the capacity to become. No one can prove that we can do any of the things we dream of doing. No one can prove that one day we shall know some of the things we now don't know but want to know. Who can be sure that we shall be able to improve our human lot in the days to come? Inquirers believe that we can, nevertheless. That is their faith. Inquirers live their lives believing that here on earth we see through a glass darkly, but that we *see*; that while human knowledge is at best only a torch of smoky pine, that nevertheless we *know*. They hold that our deeds, however nobly done, will be forgotten, but that they can and they do make a difference. The religion of the open mind and heart is a "can see, can do" attitude toward knowledge, toward understanding, and toward living, while being very conscious of the limitations that hem us in.

Lewis Thomas, after bitterly denouncing our humankind for the horror and stupidity of war, now raised to the nth power by the prospect of nuclear combat, nevertheless went on to express a high regard for our species. "As evolutionary time is measured," he continued, "we only arrived here [on this planet] a few moments ago, and we have a lot of growing up to do. If we succeed, we could become a kind of collective mind for the earth, the *thought* of the earth. . . . For all our juvenility, as a species we are surely the brightest and brainiest of the earth's working parts."[5]

Clear that we humans—all of us, Liberal and traditionalist alike—are fallible, finite creatures of earth; that we do wrong, unconsciously, and all too often intentionally, the Liberal believes in the individual self nevertheless because the record shows that we can and do catch our mistakes and correct them; we can and do see the wrong we have done, and make amends for it. We can and do distinguish between wrong and right and choose the latter. We can and do expose deceit and neutralize it. The Liberals hold that we should waste no time bemoaning our mistakes and wrongdoings. We should rather rejoice in our ability to spot them and to surmount them.

But What of Me?

All well and good; in the new paradigm for religion we believe in the self, in the multiple capacities of the self, and in the reality of all that we experience. But we still have not gotten down to the question each individual self has been asking since we first gained the capacity for reflective thought. It is the question the religions of the old paradigm—Hinduism, Buddhism, Shintoism, Judaism, Christianity, Islam, and countless others—all answer, most of them satisfactorily if we can judge by the number of adherents they have won over the centuries. All religions alike tell individual believers who they (the followers) are, what their role in life is or should be, and what happens to them after death.

If we are to give up the old paradigm for religion for the new, we need to see that we have also given up the answers the old paradigm has provided to life's most basic questions. What does the new paradigm for religion offer? How important these questions are, even to people who can be counted among the inquirers, was brought home to me one night some years ago at a lecture-discussion I was conducting on these themes. A young doctor, obviously troubled, rose to speak: "I really don't care about all this stuff on questing you are talking about," he said. "I want to know the meaning of life—the meaning of *my* life. Why must I die?"

Silence fell on the room while I gathered my thoughts to answer him. It is certainly true that our human desire to perpetuate our own personal lives is a part of the religious impulse. Some say our hope somehow to live beyond the grave is the whole of it. The records our human ancestors have left behind in all parts of the globe testify to a nearly universal yearning for immortality. Apparently when we humans first became self-conscious, when we first perceived ourselves as separate entities, the hope for immortality was born.

We can of course make too much of our human yearning to continue on forever. It lies deep within us, primitive, elemental, and admittedly powerful. John Updike, in his *Self-Consciousness: Memoirs,* put it in a phrase: "It is the self as *window on the world* that we can't bear to think of shutting" (italics mine). He wrote that he could not bear "the thought of the cosmic party going on without [him]."

As the human mind opens, and our horizon widens, the center of gravity shifts. Not for all of us, but for many, and seemingly for more and more of us as time goes on. The shift is from hope for the next world to a desire to make something of this one. That means a fundamental change in our outlook in religion. The great religions of the past sought to put us at peace with the knowledge that good people will all be rewarded eventually in eternity. The new paradigm for religion shifts the emphasis from expectations after death to life here and now; from the next world to this; from heaven where all our problems will supposedly be solved to Earth where we are required to solve them ourselves.

The people who are asking "Why must I die?" have it backwards. The most important fact about life is not that it ends but that it *is*. To live is to face up to and to deal with life's present turmoil and confusion, its suffering and pain, its anxieties, traumas, and the ever-present need to decide. These are the aspects of life, together with the moments of joy, exultation, serenity, and peace that will be ours while we live.

Then the question becomes: What does the new paradigm for religion offer to the individual by which to guide the life that each of us finds ourselves living in the here and now? How shall we act? A thousand times a day it seems we must choose to do this, that, or not do anything at all. Every choice we make has within it the possibility of affecting uncounted other people for good or ill or both, often ourselves most of all. The choices we make leave us a little cleaner or slightly more soiled, a little meaner or a little more noble. How are we to make those choices? If we do not turn to God for guidance, what guidance can a paradigm based on inquiry offer?

Traditional religion, Christianity in particular, assured the believer that she/he is a child of God who, in turn, will care for us and keep us from harm in all the vicissitudes of life. The passage from the New Testament most often cited to support this view is taken from the Sermon on the Mount in Matthew's Gospel. A central part of it reads: "Look at the birds of the air; they neither sow nor reap nor gather into barns, and yet your heavenly Father feeds them. Are you not of more value than they? . . . Consider the lilies of the field, how they grow; they neither toil nor spin; yet I tell you even Solomon in all his glory was not arrayed like one of these. But if God so clothes the grass of the field, which today is alive and tomorrow is thrown into the oven, will he not much more clothe you, O men of little faith? . . . What man of you, if his son asks him for a loaf, will give him a stone? Or if he asks for a fish will give him a serpent? If you then who are evil know how to give good gifts to your children, how much more will your Father who is in heaven give good things to those who ask him?"[6]

Citing proof texts does not usually take us far, however, and it does not in this case. Luke's Gospel contains most of the teachings in the Sermon on the Mount.[7] Often Luke and Matthew contain nearly identical lines. Yet frequently they are quite different. In a passage wholly absent from Matthew's Gospel, Luke reports Jesus asking his hearers why they are unable to read the signs of the times. You can read the signs of the weather, he tells them. You can accurately predict what is coming. "Why do you not judge for yourselves what is right?"[8] It is the question the people of the new paradigm for religion are always asking. Isn't it really up to us? Given a choice on proof texts, the question in Luke's Gospel is the text the inquirer would choose. Judge for yourself. That is to say, it is really up to you.

The inquirer would say that traditional religion offers a solution to life's problems many of its own people do not really accept and live by. A story that comes to us from the Netherlands illustrates the point. Worldwide, the Dutch are known as those remarkable people who for centuries have lived behind dikes they have built that keep the North Sea at bay. A Dutch children's story, repeated worldwide, tells us of a little boy who a long time ago saw a leak in the dike, stuck his finger in the hole, and stopped the flow of water before it could tear the dike open and flood the land. True or false, legend or myth, the story is told and retold, not only to illustrate the Dutch spirit but as a powerful parable. Its moral is plain: the difference one person can make.

The religious philosophy implied in the story is also plain. It was not a miraculous Divine intervention that saved the Dutch people from an impending disaster, it was the alertness and courage of a little boy. The moral of the tale is what one person can accomplish, even a very young person. You, even you, like the little Dutch boy, can make a difference. Sometimes, if you are lucky enough to be in the right place at the right time, and if you are alert enough and quick to act, you, even you, can make a very great difference in what goes on around you.

The new paradigm for religion in its view of the cosmic status of the individual is opposite to the lilies of the field doctrine of traditional religion. This view is not based upon theology. It is grounded in the conditions of life as we find ourselves living it. We are on our own. We humans, no less than the birds, the lilies, and the grass, have to labor for the good things in life and for the necessities as well.

Stephen Jay Gould draws the same conclusion from his studies of the evolution of life, of which we humans are a part. From the beginning we humans have taken ourselves too seriously, he suggests. We are not God's crowning achievement, at the end of an incredible period of creativity. We humans are but an accident of biological history. In a 1989 book on the meaning of an extraordinary fossil bed in Canada known as the Burgess Shale, Gould reviews the enormous decimation of life that occurred in the Cambrian era some 550 million years ago. "Wind the tape of life back to [those] times, and let it play again," he says. "If Pikaia (the world's first known chordate) does not survive in the replay, [humans, descended from them as we are] are wiped out of future history—all of us from shark to robin to orangutan. And I don't think that any handicapper, given [Cambrian] evidence as known today, would have granted us very favorable odds for the persistence of Pikaia."[9]

Gould surmised that mammalian life, including human life, would in all probability not exist on this planet today, but for the fact that the chordate Pikaia, the earliest creature known to have a backbone, managed to survive when so many other forms of life perished back in Cambrian time. From this set of facts Gould did not hesitate to draw the conclusion to which the evidence points.

"And so, if you wish to ask the question of the ages—Why do humans exist?—a major part of the answer . . . must be: because Pikaia survived the Burgess decimation. . . . I do not think any 'higher' answer can be given. . . . We are the offspring of history and must establish our own [path in the universe]—one indifferent to our suffering and, therefore, offering us maximum freedom to thrive or fail." The inquirer concurs. We learn what to believe about ourselves by studying ourselves, the planet Earth on which we dwell, and the universe beyond it, not by updating Genesis or by seeking deeper meanings in its stories.

Notes

1. Marvin Minsky, *The Society of the Mind* (New York: Simon & Schuster, 1985), p. 39.

2. Susan Krieger, *Social Science and the Self: Personal Essays on an Art Form* (New Brunswick, N.J: Rutgers University Press, 1991), p. 2.

3. Ibid.

4. Ralph Waldo Emerson, *Essays* (New York: Thomas Nelson & Sons), pp. 39ff.

5. Lewis Thomas, *The Fragile Species: Notes of an Earth Watcher* (New York: Charles Scribner's Sons, 1992), p. 135.

6. Matthew 6:26–7:11.

7. Luke 11 and 12.

8. Luke 12:57.

9. Stephen Jay Gould, *Wonderful Life* (New York: W. W. Norton & Co., 1989), p. 227.

15

The Universe

From belief in the self with the limitations each of us readily acknowledges we move to the second basic article of faith in the new paradigm for religion—belief in the universe in which we find ourselves. Each of us is confronted by the world around us in all its infinite breadth, depth, variety, complexity, and incomprehensibility. That includes the billions of other selves, each more or less like us. What are we to make of it all?

Is the universe real? Or is life only a dream? An illusion? Can life really be all that it seems to be, or more than that, far beyond our wildest imaginings? Or less, or nothing? A chimera? Wisps of hope and terror in the night?

It is a basic article of faith in the new paradigm for religion that our world is in a very real sense what it appears to be. Stated negatively it means believing that we are not deceived. Life is not a dream. The world is neither an illusion nor a joke. Other people are as real as we ourselves are. What we see, hear, touch, feel, taste, and smell is not a distorted misrepresentation of the really Real. It is as accurate a representation of the Real as we humans at this state of our development are capable of grasping.

The World Is Understandable

If we declare that we believe in ourselves and in all the other selves we find around us; and if we go on to assert that the world is what it seems to be, at least to some degree, we are also saying that we

161

humans have the capacity to understand it, at least to some degree. We are saying that we humans, despite our fallibility, have the capacity to move toward truth. No one can prove that there is, in fact, any such thing as Reality, that our world is understandable, or even that it exists apart from our experiencing. To say so is a clear act of faith.

Some of the world's greatest thinkers have held that the world, as we know it, is only a shadowy replica of Reality. Plato held this opinion. So did Bishop George Berkeley in the eighteenth century. Reality exists only in the mind, Berkeley insisted. Human experience is like a dream. The common-sense people of the time snorted their incredulity, but in the end Berkeley's contemporaries had to concede that they could not prove him wrong. On the other hand, neither could anyone prove that he was right.

Faced with such a metaphysical stalemate, those who follow the new paradigm for religion ask: What then do I really know? As I look about at myself and the world, what, if anything, can I be sure of? Here I am experiencing the world around me, stretching out in all directions in both time and space. Time stretches back from this moment, spreading as it goes like the veins in a great fan. Just behind me are the events in my life of a moment ago. Next are those of five minutes ago. Looking further back I come to breakfast time; before that, my waking and rising, then yesterday, then last week, last month, and last year.

Soon history takes up the task of stating things I do not know at firsthand, things which I have read about and those I once knew, and have since forgotten. Back of all that stretches time as far as the human mind can conceive it, back to events about which I have heard or read, and back beyond them to Earth's story as science has reconstructed it, back to the origins of the universe itself.

Time also stretches out from me into the future, also endlessly. As I look ahead things grow increasingly dark and mysterious. In the future lies hope, but also fear. What will happen to our children? We know some of the good things that might come. But we also know that we humans have developed the capacity to destroy ourselves and make the planet Earth uninhabitable. How are we to avoid such a calamity? How are we to secure the future from the knaves and fools in our midst? Do any questions haunt us more than these as we stand in the here and now where we are, looking ahead?

Space is as endless and as mysterious as time. For me, as for everyone else, space begins with my self-consciousness, with the body, where my self-consciousness resides. I am my head, arms, legs, and torso, and the forearm and hand with which I am writing. Beyond whatever I am are the pen, the paper, the desk on which it rests, the room where the desk stands, the house which contains the room, the land around the house, the town where it was built, the state, the nation, the planet, the solar system, our galaxy, the universe, and whatever may be conceived as lying beyond that, out where space and time become one.

Pointing in the other direction, inward rather than outward, lies the unseen world revealed to us by the microscope, until, again with the aid of the natural scientists, we move down into the world of molecules and atoms, electrons, neutrinos, quarks, and whatever lies beyond them.

Even that does not complete the picture. Each of us, beginning with the self, beginning where we are, also looks out upon the totality of our experience, expanding as do all the other dimensions of the known as we move from the here and now toward the unknown. We begin with immediate experience, sight, taste, smell, and touch. Slowly we develop instruments by which to extend, enlarge, and enhance our experience: glasses, telescopes, microscopes, photography, amplifiers, and the rapidly expanding field of electronics. We then evolve patterns of thought by which to understand it all. Striving to cope with the torrent of experiences that now pour in upon us, we reach out for new concepts by which to relate the elements we perceive to one another. As best we can we tie them together into a single totality. Still there is so much that eludes us, so much that we but dimly see and barely understand. Yet we move eagerly on, excited, often frustrated, but often rewarded from time to time with stunning insight, sometimes overwhelmed by the wonder and glory of it all.

Who or What Is God?

When we have tried with all that is within us to understand ourselves and our world we are brought willy-nilly to the most comprehensive and fundamental concept the human mind can formulate, the idea of God. Who or what is the Deity? A thousand names come to mind. Ten thousand definitions will not complete the answer to this question. In the West in the nineteenth century it became common to say simply "God is Love." Recently it has become commonplace to delineate Deity as a Power—"That Which Moves Us to Righteousness, Mercy, Justice, Honor, and Lovingkindness."

Charles Hartshorne, a leading proponent of process philosophy, published a hefty volume in 1953, compiling the best thinking of the greatest philosophers about God. It proved to be not only very dull reading but also inconclusive. What can we say on so vast a subject in a few paragraphs, or a fifty-foot bookshelf? Let me illustrate the problem from the writings of my own favorite philosopher, Alfred North Whitehead. A god who is in some sense personal lies at the heart of his grand speculative scheme wherein all knowledge and understanding are brought together in a single unity. Cannot that satisfy the critical mind? The weakness in such a concept has long since been pointed out by religious traditionalists. Who could be moved spiritually by Whitehead's Deity, they ask. What persuasive power can be found in an abstraction described as "the ideal world of conceptual harmonization"?

In the concluding portion of Whitehead's *Religion in the Making*, ask yourself wherein there lies any compulsion to believe in the intellectual construct he develops there. Perhaps Whitehead, in the profundity of his thought, is centuries ahead of his time. Perhaps the concepts he has developed in his several writings point to an Ultimate Reality that humanity will one day recognize and acknowledge.

But perhaps not. Certainly as of the present moment Whitehead's God is but one of many consistent, competent, comprehensive concepts by which humanity has sought to grasp the nature of Ultimate Reality. That is far from saying, however, that one believes in the reality of Whitehead's concept, or in the concept to which any of the other great philosophers have come as they completed their grand all-inclusive conceptual schemes. Possible? Yes. Probable? To some, perhaps. Compelling, as belief must be to find a place in a religious belief structure? Not at all.

All of this I find myself driven to say, although Whitehead was the greatest teacher I ever had and his thought has influenced me more than that of any other writer. Knowing him personally a little, however, I sense no incongruity in adding that, asked the questions we are considering here, he might well have responded that consistency and clarity are paramount in thinking of any kind. We cannot change the conclusions to which clear, consistent thinking brings us when we don't happen to like them. But if we find that we mistrust our conclusions we must then go back over our train of thought and find the soft spot in it. Speaking personally, I never felt that the Deity who was the ultimate, final, and central segment in Whitehead's philosophical system was the God who lived in his great heart.

Transcendence

In the nineteenth century the Liberals, in their attempt to bring their thinking about the really Real into line with the highest standards of truth-seeking, turned to the idea of transcendence. Many still do. Wilfred Cantwell Smith, for example, a leading authority in the comparative history of religion, argues that "there has been throughout history and across the world a general human awareness of transcendence; and a general human propensity to perceive it, and to express and to nurture the awareness of it, in and through specific forms. Transcendence," he continued, "has had many and diverse human expressions in quite varied words, concepts, images, forms." But the point of it all is that "the reality to which our experience of transcendence endeavors to refer transcends our apprehension of it."[1]

The trouble with an idea like transcendence made into "The Transcendent" is that it does not stand up well under close critical examination. Believing in the reality of our world and in the validity of our experience of it means believing that we can understand it, at least to some degree. That in turn involves a yet more basic idea. It means believing that the cosmos has a pattern, which in turn means believing that ultimately the cosmos is a unity. All the parts go together. In the end they are consistent with one another and with the whole. But if all the parts, taken together, make a cohesive pattern, it follows further that ours is not and cannot be a two-storied universe. In the new paradigm for religion the idea of a two-storied universe creates an insolvable problem. Two fundamental questions arise: First, where is the evidence for a "Wholly Other" or a "Transcendent"? Second, if the universe is truly a universe, none is possible.

In the eyes of the new paradigm for religion, the concept of God as "The Transcendent" is the last refuge of the beleaguered Liberal. If you want to hold to traditional theology while fully accepting the standards of the Western intellectual tradition, you may seem to be able to do so with a Deity who is transcendent. This the Liberals dearly want to do. They openly accept the findings of science. All their lives they have held to the stringent standards of scholarship developed in the universities of the West. The very vagueness of the concept of transcendence seems to make it possible for them to hold to the Western intellectual tradition and to the God of that tradition, both at the same time.

Changing God's Name

Nevertheless we are forced to ask this question: What does it accomplish to take the idea of "transcendence," make it a noun, and spell it with a capital letter? It only pushes the argument one step further back. What is it that transcends the limits of human experience? If something lies beyond the limits of human experience, how can we know what it is? If we feel that we know what it is, how is it any longer beyond the realm of human experience?

If "The Transcendent" transcends our human ability to understand it, we have to concede that we don't know—in fact cannot know— what we are talking about. That well may be. But if that is the case should we go on trying? There may be no more important topic we can address than the existence and nature of God. But does not the discussion become pointless if we declare as we begin that we cannot answer the questions we are asking?

To say that God is the Transcendent is not to solve the problem of the Ultimate but only to restate it. Questions as to who and what the Divine is, and how the Divine operates are not answered in this way. In the new paradigm for religion "The Transcendent" substituted for "Deus" does not make the Divine more comprehensible, more believable, or more real.

In the same vein, many a contemporary theologian argues that religion itself is something set apart. "Truth is known through love, awe and worship," wrote Stephen R. H. Clark of Liverpool University. "God does not belong to the class of existent things but is above all things, may even be above existence itself. To quote John of Damascus, an eighth-century theologian, . . . God is 'that uncategorized perfection whose existence is either absolutely necessary or totally impossible.' "[2]

With a definition like that we confront another form of the unanswerable argument. Clark may be right and he may not be. We cannot say. But we can say that before he starts, he has removed his proposition from human discourse, where we shall have to leave it. There is no away to get at a statement that concerns what is "above all things" and "beyond existence itself."

Discussing these questions with my fellow ministers, I find that most of them are seeking an ultimately theological basis for their thinking. The concept of "The Transcendent" does this for many of them. It provides an object, and thus an explanation for the genuinely religious feelings most of us have. The idea is sufficiently inexact to allow for the many varying concepts of the Deity they hold. It makes for the unity in diversity all alike desire.

Speaking personally, however, I find it difficult to distinguish between today's "Transcendent" and yesterday's "Wholly Other." The "Mysterium Tremendum" of Rudolph Otto, the "God Beyond God" and the "Ground of Being" of Paul Tillich, the "Unmoved Mover" of Aristotle—none of these solve the age-old problem of the existence or of the nature of Deity. Changing God's name too easily becomes a device by which we can continue to say, "I believe in God," when the Ultimate in which we really believe is far removed from the concept we think we hold when we make that ancient and sacred declaration.

Do You Believe in God?

The gravest problem for the people of the new paradigm for religion is that all too often the ground shifts at this point. Asking questions like those we have been considering, the inquirer is charged with being an unbeliever. We dealt with this problem briefly in chapter 12, but it recurs in many guises and we have now to enlarge upon it here.

Merely to ask questions about the concept of God—whether as the Transcendent or as Immanent, as a Power or as Love—is, for most people, to deny that God exists. Yet it is no such thing. It is only to say, "Here is an article of faith which has so many meanings today that it has lost all real meaning for me." If I ask what others mean when they say "God," I do not deny the truth of the idea. I am trying to pin down what others mean by what they are saying. To be specific, the new paradigm for religion does not find the concept of God as "The Transcendent" helpful or meaningful. It does not enable us to understand our world any better than we already do. But this is far from saying that our sense of the presence of that which transcends human understanding is not very real, for it is.

What are those who talk about God actually talking about? This is what the inquirer wants to know. When the traditionalists classify people as believers and unbelievers, they are separating people from one another on the basis of their several differing theological systems. They are dividing people from one another according to the language they use to state their beliefs about Ultimate Reality. Theists are people who make God-language central. Inquirers are people who do not.

Is God-language or the lack of it so important? The critical mind would insist that our theories of Reality are not basic enough to justify our separating people from one another in religion or in any other aspect of life. If people are to be set apart, the inquirer would ask that we do so according to the ideals they hold and how far they live by them.

"God" would seem to be ill-served by many of his/her would-be defenders. The traditionalists seem to care more about the name than the concept. Often their concepts appear to differ little if any from those of the inquirers. In the new paradigm for religion the existence of God is by no means denied. No more basic idea has ever formed in the human mind. For the inquirer the concern is for the meaning of the God-idea. In the new paradigm for religion there is a burning desire to cut through today's beclouded theological language to a clarity and consistency of statement and concept that religion once had but now seems to have lost. That clarity and consistency can only be achieved, the inquirer maintains, by making religion completely and fully a part of the Western intellectual tradition.

Inquirers see most, if not all of the traditional attempts to save God from the questioners as falling short of the mark. But pointing out those shortcomings does not turn questioners into unbelievers. Many, if not most inquirers have the same religious yearnings the defenders of tradition have. The yearning to understand the Ultimate is universal. It is with inquirers no less than the most stouthearted defender of traditional religion. Inquirers are not doubters; they are believers. But they do not believe in the deities of modern theology, patched together as they are out of ancient visions and contemporary science and philosophy. Their point, which the defenders so often miss, is simple: It is that too much of the defense the defenders offer is seriously flawed. It does make questioners into believers. It makes would-be believers into doubters, and doubters into unbelievers.

Edith Sitwell wrote:

Said the Sun to the Moon—when you are but a lonely white crone,
And I a dead king in my golden armor somewhere in a dark wood,
Remember only this of our hopeless love
That never till Time is done
Will the fire of the heart and the fire of the mind be one.[3]

Those who follow the new paradigm for religion will nod in agreement with the thrust of these lines. They will not deny either the power or the importance of the fire of the heart. But they would add that we shall have a better world in which to dwell when we learn that the fire of the heart must be tempered by the fire of the mind. We know to our sorrow how tragically mistaken the heart can be (as can the mind). Both are essential. Each is needed to temper the other. To illumine and to warm the human spirit, the two fires, uninhibited, must be permitted to consume us, both at the same time.

In the end, those who embrace the new paradigm for religion have no quarrel with those for whom the idea of The Transcendent is a solution to the theological problem. Their quarrel is with those who insist that you cannot have a satisfactory philosophy of life without the Transcendent or an equivalent concept at the head of it. The quarrel is with the dogmatists who think there can be no moral imperative apart from an Absolute or Almighty from whom the Moral Law emanates. The quarrel is with those who maintain that the idea of a Wholly Other who makes these things possible is essential if one is to know wonder, feel excitement, behold beauty, or experience enchantment. The quarrel is with those who insist that any answer to questions about belief in the universe must include Deity in one form or another. Inquirers insist that that question, given our present knowledge, remains open for discussion.

To a high degree the contemporary argument in religion comes down in the end to a single question: Is religion something separate and apart from all other human experience, thought and activity, or is religion an integral part of the whole of life? Inquirers maintain that when we stand in the presence of the sacred, when we confront the ineffable, experience transcendence, move into the realm of the spirit, we are not in an area of thought and activity different in kind from everything else. Religion is not a domain where the standards we apply in all other aspects of life may be set aside.

In the new paradigm for religion life and thought, experience and knowledge are all of a piece. The inquiring mind and the open heart insist that calling something "religious" does not exempt it from the standards of judgment we abide by in all the other aspects of life. The faith of Enlightenment people is not arbitrary. It is derived from and rests upon the vast structure of thought the West has built. The open mind and the open heart want to make religion an integral part of this structure. Their goal is to make religion as believable as science, as persuasive as astrophysics, and its call for righteousness as powerful as the pull of gravity.

Metaphysics, Philosophy, Theology, and Religion

What is the ultimate question? Traditional religion might answer: What is the nature of God? The inquirer would say the ultimate question is: What is the really Real? What is the Totality of Things? We humans, all of us, in all places and times and cultures, have been striving to delineate the nature of the self, the nonself, the world each of us confronts, and the ultimate meaning of it all. In traditional religion that is theology, the science of God. In philosophy it is speculation about the natural world and about us humans who dwell within it. In the new paradigm for religion both are the same. Both religion and philosophy are seen as sincere attempts to delineate the nature of the universe as completely and as accurately as possible.

The new paradigm for religion holds that the best current theology or philosophy or metaphysical system will one day reveal its own errors and limitations. However imaginatively wrought, and however carefully worked out, each will eventually be replaced by a clearer, more profound set of concepts, the result of broadening and deepening human understanding worldwide. There is nothing inevitable about it to be sure, but thus far human history seems to have proceeded according to this formula.

As the new paradigm for religion views the situation, the "war" between religion and science will not conclude with victory for one side or the other, nor with a compromise between the two. It will end only when we see that neither can ever be completely right. The best amalgam of the two will not be right either. The answer to the problem of philosophy and theology—the problem of ulti-mates—for our time, and probably for all time, lies in the continuing accumulation of knowledge and understanding held with an open mind and heart, whereby we are able to see ever more deeply into the nature of things. The open mind and heart would invite one and all to give up the old paradigm for religion and accept the new as numbers of people have already done, most without quite realizing that they have done so.

Notes

1. Wilfred Cantwell Smith, "Transcendence," *Harvard Divinity School Bulletin* (Fall 1988): 1.

2. Stephen R. L. Clark, quoted in *Context* (December 1, 1986): 6.

3. Edith Sitwell, *The Canticle of the Rose* (New York: Vanguard Press, 1949), p. 193.

16

The Whole Body of Knowledge

If we are to state the beliefs by which inquirers understand their universe and order their lives, we have much further to go. In the previous chapter we saw how quickly such an attempt degenerates into an argument about standards. As we saw in Part Two, tradition in religion in the area of ultimates is so strong that a probing into basic beliefs soon slides into a discussion of the legitimacy of what is being discussed. Deity and the vast array of concepts, practices, and institutions associated with that single, very basic concept is the problem.

Can we have nothing then but the continuing disputation so characteristic of theology? Can we or can we not formulate beliefs in the new paradigm for religion? The answer to that question is yes, we can.

Inquirers believe in the whole body of knowledge. That means they accept the information we humans have been accumulating and recording for some thousands of years. It means accepting one or another of the multiple interpretations of those meanings our human minds have developed. It means accepting metaphysical, ethical, epistemological, artistic, economic, historical, scientific knowledge of every kind, including religious knowledge.

But not in toto, and by no means absolutely; it means accepting the whole and the several parts in widely varying degrees. For always there hangs over us the cloud of our human fallibility. Accepting "knowledge" plunges us into an endless sorting and sifting process as to what is and what is not true knowledge. We continually discover errors in what passes for knowledge and we have continually to eliminate those errors. We have continually to modify what we find is only half true, half understood, misleading, or skewed.

Beyond that yet another problem looms: the whole body of knowledge the ˌman race has accumulated is inconceivably vast. It is already so great as to be literally insurmountable for any one person. How can we be said to believe all that? Nevertheless, in the new paradigm for religion we do. The inquirer accepts the whole body of knowledge for what it is, nothing more, but nothing less. Open minds and hearts have faith in the validity of the entire corpus despite its enormous size. It is accepted even while it continually grows and changes, as new knowledge is acquired, and as old errors and misconceptions are eliminated.

What and How We Believe

How can so colossal an amount of believing be managed, even by the best of us? By believing in the whole body of knowledge in the same way science does; in the same way scholars committed to Western university standards believe; in the same way people brought up in the Western intellectual tradition believe. The better the evidence all told, in every dimension, the stronger the belief; the poorer the evidence all told, and also in every dimension, the weaker the belief.

As an example, inquirers believe unquestioningly in the law of gravity. They believe it on the evidence gathered in centuries of thought and study on the problem and the way in which the concept fits into and explains so many aspects of human experience. Inquirers also believe in evolution. Modern science is now virtually unanimous in asserting that the principle of evolution explains the extraordinary proliferation of life on this planet. There is increasing agreement that evolution may explain the changing, developing universe itself. These beliefs are now held by inquirers also, again on the evidence and based on the way the concept fits so many aspects of our experience—not as an article of faith.

The scientists also believe, although less positively, in a more recently accepted theory, that of the Big Bang. There is no longer any debate among them about the fact of the force of gravitation.

They are now virtually agreed that evolution is a fact, not merely a theory. In the new paradigm for religion all three of the foregoing beliefs are held in the same way that the scientists hold them. But again, let it be stressed that these beliefs are held not as articles of faith, but on the evidence, broadly interpreted and understood.

The Creation Story

To illustrate, basic in the whole body of human knowledge is the story of creation. From time immemorial, we humans have asked: Where did the universe come from? How did things get started? Who or what did it? What keeps it all going?

Primitive people gave primitive answers to these questions. Among the many we can precisely document is the creation story of a Stone Age culture present in our world today, that of the Haida people of the Queen Charlotte Islands off the coast of western Canada. They say that the first people were discovered by a raven in a clam shell. The Judeo-Christian tradition has taught since the fifth or sixth century B.C.E. that the universe came into existence when God created the world out of nothing in six days and, as his crowning and final achievement, created two human beings, Adam and Eve, from whom the entire human race is descended.

As scholars have long since made clear, there are two creation stories in the Bible. The older and more primitive one is in Genesis 2; the later, more elaborate and sophisticated one is in Genesis 1. Fundamentalist Christians insist that these two chapters are the last word on the subject, because the Bible is God's very Word. But the problem of origins cannot be so easily solved. If Genesis 1 and 2 are the final word on the subject of universal beginnings, what are we to say about the findings contemporary science reached after generations of careful study by countless scholars in fields ranging from astronomy to zoölogy?

Valiant attempts at reconciling Genesis and scientific thinking have been made since the days of Galileo and Copernicus. In the new paradigm for religion such efforts are regarded as not merely empty, but as creating a problem where none would otherwise exist. There is no more conflict between the stories in Genesis and the scientific story of cosmic evolution than there is between Homer's *Iliad*, the Gilgamesh epic, or the Rig Veda and scientific thought. Each is an expression of the human spirit, valid for its own purposes in its own place and time. But the truth in each can be seen and appreciated only when each of them is considered in the context in which it first appeared, the purpose it was intended to serve, and the wider knowledge enjoyed by the culture in which the story first appeared.

The people of the new paradigm for religion do not do as the traditionalists do with these stories. They do not try to reinterpret ancient writings to make them useful today. For an understanding of the beginning of things they turn instead to the ablest people they can find who have addressed the problem broadly and conscientiously and who have fashioned their answers according to the strictest rules of observation, experimentation, and conceptual thinking. They turn to the astronomers, astrophysicists, cosmologists, mathematicians, and the many others who today are wrestling with these profound questions.

The growing depth and detail of our present knowledge is extraordinary. From the Haida story of a raven and the clamshell to the events in the nanoseconds immediately following the Big Bang the distance we have come in our understanding of what happened is astonishing. And we believe it. The tale today's scientists tell is believed in the new paradigm for religion because it makes sense; it is the best account of universal origins now obtainable.

And what is that story? It has been retold many times. Leon Lederman, a government research and development expert, summarizes them all succinctly as follows: "In the beginning there was a void—a curious form of vacuum, a nothingness, neither time nor space, neither stars nor planets—neither rocks nor trees, neither animals nor human beings. There were, however, in place the laws of nature, or so we believe. And these laws dictated that the curious vacuum would explode and in this initial incandescence there were created space, time, and a hot plasma of primordial particles. As the universe cooled and grew less dense, particles coagulated and forces differentiated. Pristine symmetry gave way to evolving complexity. Protons and neutrons formed, then nuclei and atoms and huge clouds of dust, which, still expanding, condensed locally here and there to form the galaxies and the stars and the planets.

"On one planet—this one, a most ordinary planet, following precise mathematics, orbiting a mediocre star, one speck on the spiral arm of a standard galaxy—turbulent landmasses and more turbulent oceans organized themselves, and out of the oceans an ooze of organic molecules reacted and built up the protein, and eventually life began. Plants and animals evolved out of simple organisms, and, in time, human beings arrived."[1]

To keep things in perspective, we might add that contemporary thinking about basics like how things began has recast the question. Today's philosophers are asking: Why is there anything at all? Why is there something rather than nothing? To ask about how things began assumes that there was a beginning. To ask why anything exists avoids that assumption. It puts us back with Descartes's root question about existence. For a real puzzler, try that one and see what you come up with. How are we to explain the fact of existence itself?

On Whom Shall We Rely?

Confronted by the stretch from Genesis to today's astrophysics, many a theologian has cried, "My God is too small!" Such an exclamation restates the problem traditional theology has to deal with at this point: a concept of deity that has constantly to be expanded to accommodate the latest scientific thinking does not inspire worship or invite belief. In answer, the inquiring mind would ask: Why start with a deity who was real to the mind of the fifth or sixth century B.C.E. and try to hold to that? The people of that time, given the knowledge they possessed, readily believed in a person-like God who created the world in six days, and who walked and talked with the first man and woman in the first garden. Can we do that? Can we successfully bring that Deity into the twentieth century? A more important question is: Need we try? Why should a twentieth-century mind be asked to settle for a Bronze Age God? In the new paradigm for religion we start as the ancients did, with the thought of the wisest and most knowledgeable people around. At that time it was the priesthood. Today it is the cosmologists. Starting with them, the problem of clinging to a Deity who is too small does not exist.

At this point the traditionalists ask: But is the new paradigm for religion really different from the old if both rely on an outside authority to tell them the truth? Traditional religion offers people the Genesis story, and invites questioners and doubters to consider the deeper meanings that can be found within it. Does the line "The earth was without form and void and darkness was on the face of the deep"[2] really differ from the essentials of the Big Bang scenario, the traditionalists ask? In both instances do not the believers rely on recognized authorities to tell them what happened at the world's beginning?

Superficially, it might seem so, but in fact the difference between the two is profound. In the new paradigm for religion putting our faith in the scientific story does not mean putting our faith in a church and then, like Augustine or Anselm, striving to believe what the church teaches, even though it may seem contrary to reason and common sense. It was the second-century churchman Tertullian who exclaimed, perhaps in desperation, "I believe because it is impossible!"

In the new paradigm for religion, when we give over to the astrophysicists, biologists, and geologists the task of explaining the origin and destiny of the universe, or the meaning of existence itself, we do so under three very important conditions not present in traditional religious faith. First, we accept only those formulations on which the experts themselves generally agree. Second, when we accept those formulations we hold them exactly as the astrophysicists, biologists, and geologists do—as the best that can be made on the existing evidence. Third, we hold our beliefs subject, always, to subsequent modification or replacement whenever a better formulation gains consensus because it is seemingly more accurate and because it more adequately explains the data from which it is derived.

In chapter 11 we noted that scientists are very clear as to what science does and what it does not do. Science does not dream up stories as to how and why things happened. Anyone can do that. Science was born when we humans began sorting out stories about how and why things happen according to our ability to verify them. Verification is the key word. Science is concerned only with stories that can be tested for validity.

For example, science has no interest in debating the Haida story of creation. But today's cosmologists have the greatest interest in attempts to prove or disprove the Big Bang story. They go further. Today they are busy dreaming up ways to find evidence to support the story or to prove it false. The latest step in this process was the space probe designed by the National Aeronautical and Space Administration of the United States, called the Cosmic Background Explorer (COBE). Its purpose was to detect, if possible, "clumpiness" in the early universe, soon after the Big Bang took place.

Why "clumpiness"? Because, the cosmologists reasoned, if the contents of space had remained uniform after the Big Bang, there would have been nothing for gravity to work on. In that case the universe would have expanded at an even rate in all directions. With no clumps anywhere, no galaxies and no stars would have formed. With clumpiness, gravity would have built larger and larger clumps everywhere and the universe as we know it in all its diversity would have become possible.

COBE revealed the presence of clumpiness in the early universe. The COBE computer simulations contained concrete evidence of it. Seeing this the scientists agreed that, on this new evidence, the Big Bang theory could be accepted as a tested scenario for the origin of our universe.

"If you're religious, it's like looking at God," exclaimed the leader of the COBE research team. "They've found the missing link," said another. "This removes the biggest remaining objection to the Big Bang."[3] The "clouds" in the COBE pictures are the largest and the oldest structures ever observed. Looking at them, many scientists are now ready to say that the Big Bang story of our beginnings has moved from theory to fact.

Awe, Wonder, Excitement!

If the cosmic ponderings being reviewed here were to be repeated ten years hence they would be different, although probably not radically so. The statements of the scientists, summing up what the astrophysicists suppose themselves to know, would be replaced by newer ones containing later refinements in scientific thought, revised in the light of the latest discoveries and the latest speculation as to what it all means. "The universe has spent billions of years writing the story of creation," one observer remarked wryly. "Humans will no doubt be trying to read it for quite some time to come."[4] Does that mean our cosmology is inevitably false? No, neither in science nor in the new paradigm for religion. In both, our cosmology is expected to grow and change as scientific knowledge increases and as our understanding of it all grows more profound. Each new explanation is in effect a new edition of the myth of creation.

Traditional theologians often assume that the fluid state of cosmology in science causes gloom and anxiety among inquirers in religion. The very opposite is the case. Inquirers in religion cannot find words adequate to convey the sense of awe, wonder, and excitement that seizes them as they contemplate the cosmos modern science is constructing. The fact that the picture is constantly growing and changing makes it seem more, not less wondrous, and more, not less believable.

Magic, wonder, and enchantment are very much in vogue today. Typical is *The Reenchantment of the World* by Morris Berman (1984). Like so many contemporary thinkers, Berman draws a sharp contrast between the thought of Descartes and his own "enchanted" outlook. He draws a harsh contrast between what he believes to be the result of Descartes's thinking and the glowing possibilities that would follow the adoption of his own. "We are forced to consider the possibility that modern science may not be epistemologically superior to the occult world view," he writes, "and that a metaphysics of participation may actually be more accurate than the metaphysics of Cartesianism."[5]

The popularity of books like Berman's testifies to our contemporary yearning for religious feeling—for a sense of awe, mystery, and wonder. What the enthusiasts for such writing fail to see is the large segment of thoughtful people who know at firsthand the experience of enchantment, but who also insist on taking a hard look at what they are enchanted with. These people are no less eager to experience enchantment than are the occult-minded, but they are concerned with the harm enchantment can do when it is lodged in folly or results from fraud.

In the new paradigm for religion people believe with the Apostle Paul that now we see through a glass darkly,[6] but they add: "We believe that we *see*, and we believe no less stoutly that tomorrow, if all goes well, we shall see better than we do today." There is nothing inevitable about it. Nevertheless our history on this planet has so far shown that belief in the possibility of a continuing although often interrupted gain in knowledge and understanding is justified. If we can keep our good sense and control the forces of destruction that now threaten us, and probably always will, our children will know more tomorrow than we do today, and our children's children will know and understand even more than that.

Reality

If we believe in the whole body of human knowledge, we believe in something so vast we cannot encompass it, this is clear. We cannot begin to state what it is that we believe. No mind can grasp all of it, nor can any group of minds. No encyclopedia can contain it. No library or system of libraries can hold it. If some massive chain of computers could be devised that could, we would still have the problem of its ever-growing and changing content. What kind of believing is that?

It is belief in Reality, the really Real, whatever that is, formulated as best we are able to formulate it in our place and time, says the inquirer. Many a traditionalist today, like the traditionalists of old, reply that at best the new paradigm for religion leaves us with a cold, somber, impersonal kind of religion that is no religion at all. At best, they say, it is one more philosophy, which will soon pass. It has no loving, caring God, and no prayer. No magic, no mystery, no beauty, no help for the helpless, no comfort when the anxiety and fear, the misery and sorrow we all must meet are more than we can bear. All the complaints against the older Liberalism are revived by the defenders of the old paradigm and flung at the defenders of the new.

Inquirers in religion, clear as to what they do and do not believe, reply that on the contrary they, too, believe in prayer as all people do, regardless of their theology or lack of it. Prayer is a natural and universal human reaction to the crises of life. True prayer—not the formal petitions drawn up by churchmen and recited in formal worship—*true* prayer is a spontaneous cry of pain when we are beset with unendurable anxiety or anguish. It is a passionate plea for help when we are helpless.

"Oh, let this pass," we cry, or "Let him (or her) live and not die," we pray. "Let me somehow bear this pain," we breathe desperately. "Let me stand up to whatever lies ahead! Let me be true to myself. Let me not give in despite the pressure—or temptation—to do wrong." Which of us has not uttered such a prayer in our extremity? We may cry, "God help me!" or we may murmur simply, "Let me be brave." The language we choose does not matter. Prayer is universal. Only the ignorant can claim never to have prayed. Inquirers, alert as they are to the realities of life, do not do less. In life's extremities they, too, pray and no less fervently than anyone else.

The difference between the inquirer and the traditionalist on this point is not who does and who does not pray. The difference is between how each would describe what is happening in the act of prayer. To see the issue clearly, ask yourself: "When I pray, what am I doing? Am I calling upon an Almighty Power to come down from heaven and rearrange the affairs of earth for my benefit? Do I really expect that? Am I asking for a miracle?" That is what prayer amounts to when we ask God to intervene on our behalf.

Or contrarily, ask yourself: "When I pray, am I simply crying out in desperation for help in a situation I have not the strength to meet alone? Am I doing more than attempting to deal with an emergency that overwhelms me, with no thought as to whence or how such extra powers can come to me?" There is but one answer to such a question. In the crushing moment when life wrings from us a spontaneous cry for help, we are not thinking about theological questions. That may come later, perhaps not at all. On this point, but one thing is clear. The theology of prayer differs, often wildly, from person to person. The fact that we pray does not. Prayer belongs to us all as humans.

The Inquirer's Prayer

Yes, inquirers pray as all people pray, and few have an aversion to the calmer type of utterance we associate with formal worship. But they ask that on such occasions the language of the prayer make it clear to the worshiper what is happening. Inquirers might well prefer the word "aspiration" to describe how they feel about it. The point can best be illustrated with the prayer of an ancient Stoic. It was quoted by the British classicist Gilbert Murray in his *Four Stages of Greek Religion,* published before World War I. One Eusebius, a late Ionic Platonist, wrote it. Nothing is now known of him, not even the date at which he lived. Thus we can judge his prayer on its merits, free of the religious loyalties that might otherwise cloud our judgment. The prayer reads:

"May I be no one's enemy, and may I be the friend of that which is eternal and abides. May I never quarrel with those nearest me; and if I do may I be reconciled quickly. May I never devise evil against any one; and if any devise evil against me may I escape uninjured, and without the need of hurting them. May I love, seek, and attain only that which is good. May I wish for the happiness of all and may I envy none. May I never rejoice in the ill fortune of one who has wronged me. When I have done or said what is wrong may I never wait for the rebuke of others, but always rebuke myself until I make amends. May I win no victory that harms either me or my opponent. May I reconcile friends who are wroth with one another. May I, to the extent of my power, give all needful help to my friends and to all who are in want. May I never fail a friend in danger. When visiting those in grief may I be able by gentle and healing words to soften their pain. . . . May I always keep tame that which rages within me. . . . May I accustom myself to be gentle, and never angry with anyone because of circumstances. May I never discuss who is wicked and what wicked things they may have done, but know good people and follow in their footsteps."[7]

This prayer can be cast in traditional form by simply addressing it to God. But it can be offered with equal effect—with greater effect for the inquirer—by using it just as Eusebius wrote it over two thousand years ago. I, myself, have done so many times in the course of conducting formal worship in church. Gilbert Murray, after quoting the prayer, commented: "How unpretending it is and yet how searching! And in the whole there is no petition for any material blessing, and—most striking of all—it is addressed to no 'personal God.' It is pure prayer."[8]

Prayers like that of Eusebius are not for everyone. Vast numbers of people center their faith in a Deity who, when called upon by the deserving, will intervene in human affairs on their behalf. Increasing numbers today do not. Yet they find that the need for strength in times of crisis is answered, we know not how, when in our human weakness we cry out in despair. Inquirers know that this is so because so many of them have found great strength when, with a whole heart, they have prayed in this fashion. As to the theology of it, they are content to let those who wish to enter the lists and contend with one another as to what it all means theologically. For the rest of us, they say, let the question go unanswered as it must, given the limits of our present knowledge.

What we think about prayer is apt to be the same as what we think about God. With both there is often a wide discrepancy between what we think we believe and what in our heart of hearts we really hold. Such beliefs are often like Christmas tree ornaments—beautiful to behold, but of little substance and easily shattered. A belief easily spoken aloud but not held in the heart is a delusion. In times of crises, when beliefs that are deep and strong are needed, a prayer resting on a theology we do not really believe leaves us defenseless. Sensing that this is so, the inquirer insists that we face up boldly to the question of our true beliefs. In times of trial only the beliefs that are held deep down inside can sustain us. In the fundamental choices for living it is not the beliefs we easily recite, but those we really hold that determine what we do.

The Really Real

In the end it is Reality that we seek. We believe in Reality, not because some authority has told us we should, but because we must. We have no other choice. Reality is what is. It is so basic a concept that the dictionary defines it negatively—by what it is not. Reality is not artificial, not fraudulent, not illusory. Reality is not something apparent. Reality is what is genuine.

If we believe in Reality because we can do no other, our question is not the one the religions are asking. It is not: What do I believe, or what should I believe? Our question is: What is it that compels my believing because I cannot escape it? Why do I believe in *that* idea of Reality rather than some other? These are the questions we must ask. These are the questions we must answer.

In the whole body of knowledge we humans are accumulating we shall find our answers. And if what we find seems inadequate, if today's whole body of knowledge is not enough to satisfy us, we need only recall that we today know more than our forebears did yesterday, and that if we continue, our children will know even more tomorrow. Can we not be content with that? For the inquirer, the answer is we can, we do, we must, and it is enough.

Notes

1. Leon M. Lederman, "Science Education, Science, and American Culture," *Key Reporter* (Winter 1991–92): 9.
2. Genesis 1:2.
3. *Time* (May 4, 1992): 62.
4. Corey S. Powell, "The Golden Age of Cosmology," *Scientific American* (July 1992): 22.
5. Morris Berman, *The Reenchantment of the World* (Toronto: Bantam Books, 1984), p. 127.
6. 1 Corinthians 13:12.
7. Gilbert Murray, *The Five Stages of Greek Religion* (Boston: Beacon Press, 1951), p. 197. This is the revised edition of *Four Stages of Greek Religion* (1913).
8. Ibid., p. 198.

17

Others

When we are asked to state what we believe in religion, we are not being asked to state our beliefs about everything. We are being asked to state our most basic beliefs about ourselves and the universe. These statements are articles of faith. They are deeply held beliefs. We live by them but cannot prove them because they are too basic to be defined by anything else. Three beliefs of this character in the new paradigm for religion have now been formulated: belief in the self, belief in the universe, and belief in the whole body of knowledge.

In the creation stories of traditional religion and in those of science, we have an example of what belief about the universe means. What comparable beliefs about people other than ourselves are held in the new paradigm for religion? In philosophical language, we are now moving from metaphysics and epistemology to ethics. On what ground do the ethics of the new paradigm for religion rest? What are some of its most basic principles? How do we know they are valid? What would compel people to obey them?

The Golden Rule

To begin with the self is to move immediately to other selves—to the people around us. Each of our fellow humans is, in a general sense, a replica of every other. The very basic experiences, capacities, needs, and aspirations we find in ourselves can be found in everyone else. Individuals will differ by degree, of course. Nevertheless, we have little doubt that for the most part, what we see, others see;

what we feel, they feel; our loves are their loves and vice versa; our hates are theirs and theirs are ours. So, too, with our strengths and weaknesses. The mistakes that we make, others make also. Our joys are theirs; our hopes are theirs; our needs are theirs; our prejudices, jealousies, dissimulation, cruelty, and greed are theirs, too.

In the new paradigm for religion, then, what I ask for myself, I must ask for you. In all reason, logic, and conscience I cannot do less. By what principle could I seek privileges for myself which I would not then be bound to seek for you? To recognize the fact of my commonality with other people is to lay upon myself the obligation to do for them what I would like them to do for me.

Saying this, I find myself on very familiar ground. Recognizing the fact of my commonality with all other people and the moral obligation that follows from it, I have stated the Golden Rule, which in one form or another has emerged in all the great religions of the world. In Christianity it reads, "Whatsoever ye would that anyone should do to you, do ye even so to them."[1] Immanuel Kant, the German philosopher of the Enlightenment period, formulated the principle in philosophical language: "So act that whatever you do can become universal law." Kant called his formulation the "Categorical Imperative," meaning a rule that has no exceptions. To state it another way, anything you do that cannot always be done by anyone anywhere is immoral. Cheating, lying, deceiving, injuring, depriving, hurting anyone in any way, dominating or enslaving other people— none of these can be made universal. A society based upon fraud will disintegrate into anarchy. A society based upon force is inevitably unjust. Dominance, by its very nature, is for the few, not the many. On the other hand, societies based upon truth, reliability, trust, kindliness, and the goal of true equality will grow strong and prosper. All others have built in self-destruction at their core.

Self-Restraint

We cannot list the virtues to be expected in a person who tries to live by the Golden Rule. There are too many of them. The virtues are too varied, and too interrelated to be encapsulated in a list. One requiring special mention, however, is self-restraint. The ability to control one's self in accordance with a set of higher principles is central to the practice of many particular virtues. Today it is among the most neglected of them.

John F. (Lord) Moulton, the nineteenth-century English jurist, in an oft-quoted aphorism, once said, "The measurement of a civilization is the degree of its obedience to the unenforceable." It was a very insightful way of putting the principle of self-restraint in its social context, where alone it has meaning. No civilization can stand if its people obey the law only when they are afraid of getting caught if they don't. Self-restraint lies at the heart of every society. It rises out of the recognition of our commonality with other people. It is the first step in living by the Golden Rule. Out of your own system of moral principles you, of your own accord, hold back from doing those things that hurt other people.

In the mid 1980s, when several cases of fraud in science came to light at the same time, *Scientific American* published an essay dealing with this problem. It illustrates a major flaw in our mores today. Discussing fraud in science, the editor found two theories of its origin: "One blames human nature," he wrote, "the other blames the circumstances in which modern research scientists work."[2] He is right on both counts, but from a moral standpoint he is dead wrong in the conclusion he reaches. The editor would eliminate fraud in science by changing the "circumstances in which modern research scientists work."

There is no doubt that today's system puts scientists under very great pressure to produce and publish original work. It is true that the system ought to be changed. Such a high degree of pressure creates the temptation to stretch the data and exaggerate the results attained. Nevertheless, to blame the system rather than the person is to relieve the individual of moral responsibility. A moral system sets standards we accept and obey voluntarily, regardless of the pressures that may be upon us. Such pressures always are present in one form or another. We are not excused from holding to our standards because they are high or because others are not doing so. Mores mean nothing if we conform to them only when it is easy, but fall down when the competition is strong. Certainly we should construct systems that induce moral rather than immoral behavior. But the best system invites deviant behavior on the part of those who do not have the capacity for self-restraint. In the new paradigm for religion the moral person holds to high principle, even when the going is impossibly hard, as it is in today's highly competitive scientific community.

As a second example, in the United States today the Food and Drug Administration (FDA) is under constant and ever mounting criticism from all quarters. It is charged that the FDA does not sufficiently test products manufactured in this country, nor does it sufficiently police the manner in which they are offered to the consumer. The widest variety of products, from cancer cures to baby food, are frequently mislabeled, too often adulterated, and offered to a trusting public unable to protect itself from carefully crafted deceit.

Loud, long, and continuous are the accusations of the FDA's neglect and inaction. But seldom does anyone rise in wrath against the established, reputable manufacturers and ask how in good conscience they can deliberately confuse and mislead the public as they do today in their manufacturing and labeling practices. Who, besides a few outspoken consumer groups, demands to know how food and medicine producers can put the health and welfare of the public at risk with adulterated and/or mislabeled products and not hang their heads in shame on account of it? Have they no standards of self-restraint? Can't they restrain their avarice?

An American magazine called *Success* announced on the cover of its March 1994 issue an article on "The Art of Deceit." The article and an editorial explaining it show what is wrong with Western culture today, in particular American culture.[3] We no longer seem to be aware of the values that made us great, and so we do not honor them or teach them to our children as our parents and grandparents taught them to us.

The editor of *Success* apparently thought the ancient Eastern tradition of treachery was a great idea. Its counterpart, the view that Western openness and fair play are naive, struck him with equal force. The result: a cover story in a widely read magazine "for today's entrepreneurial mind," advocating deceit.

The art of deception is *not* a great new idea. It is the opposite. It is a reversion to primitive ways most Westerners suppose we have outgrown and are still trying to surmount. Short-term deceit may well give the deceiver an advantage. Everyone knows that. But we also know that long-term deceit is destructive. The West, the United States in particular, grew to greatness because it built a social structure based not on deceit but its opposite, trust. Are we such fools that we are now about to reinvent deceit, and destroy the great society our forbearers bequeathed to us?

Empathy

Truly moral people not only avoid hurting others, they try to help others in every way they can. Truly moral people have a capacity for empathy. They can and do put themselves in the place of others. They are able to see things as other people see them, feel what they feel, think what they think, and sense what they yearn for. Empathy evokes a feeling of tenderness and concern within moral people, which in turn moves them to help the helpless wherever and whenever they can.

To pin down these principles we turn to the world of poetry where alone, except for sacred texts, we find them stated with sufficient clarity and force. In 1925 Vachel Lindsay in "Johnny Appleseed's Hymn" wrote with profound feeling for the world's unfortunate:

> Let not young souls be smothered out before
> They do quaint deeds and fully flaunt their pride.
> It is the world's one crime its babes grow dull.
> Its poor are ox-like, limp and leaden-eyed.
> Not that they starve, but starve so dreamlessly.
> Not that they sow, but that they seldom reap.
> Not that they serve, but have no gods to serve.
> Not that they die, but that they die like sheep.[4]

More than a century earlier William Blake, in his "Milton," had shown not merely sympathy for the downtrodden but an all-consuming desire to help them. Beholding the "dark, satanic mills" then becoming a blight on Britain's landscape and upon her people, Blake wrote:

> Bring me my Bow of burning gold!
> Bring me my Arrows of desire!
> Bring me my Spear! O clouds unfold!

Bring me my Chariot of fire!
I will not cease from Mental Fight,
    Nor shall my Sword sleep in my hand,
Till we have built Jerusalem
    In England's green and pleasant land.[5]

Unfortunately, there seems to be no limit to the aspects of evil we might draw upon to illustrate what moral action means in life as we live it. Two more examples must suffice. Either, by itself, is sickening enough to drive the point home. Both, taken together, force us to face the depths to which human depravity can sink. And yet incredibly, hope and promise for the future can rise from it all.

Human Sacrifice

We turn first to an ancient practice too horrible to contemplate, yet only recently abandoned: that of human sacrifice. The reasoning that justified such ceremonies apparently rose from our human hunger for homage. The gods demanded homage just as we humans do, it was supposed. Sacrifice was thought to be particularly impressive and more so when it was costly to those who offered it. The higher the cost the higher the degree of devotion it was thought to signify. A very great sacrifice indicated very great devotion. The highest possible sacrifice was, of course, that of human life. So far awry did primitive thinking go.

What explains our lust for the ceremonial killing of our fellow humans, or even that of animals? How do we account for a culture like that of the Maya in Central America in which the apex of their religious ceremonial was human sacrifice performed for the multitudes, at the top of a high temple erected for the purpose? How do we explain the medieval *auto-da-fé*, where heretics were routinely burned at the stake by the decree of churchmen, to the glory of God and the delectation of the multitudes?

Coming to our own time we must ask, if we are honest with ourselves, how are we to explain the current popularity of horror stories and pictures that pour out upon us today in a torrent in novels and detective stories, movies, television, and home videos? For the critical mind there is but one explanation. We are not far from the jungle, any of us. On the time scale of our planet, short as it is in a universe some 15 billion years old measured by Earth's time scale, right behind us is the jungle. There death and dismemberment, blood and gore were a part of daily life. Should we not expect, then, that there lurks in the best of us a hidden yearning for the old terrors? Today, in imagination, we view those bloody scenes with horror, some of us with much more horror than others. But the wonder is not the secret enjoyment of murder and mayhem among so many of us. The wonder is the degree to which some of us cannot endure pain and suffering in pictures or in life.

Post-Traumatic Stress Disorders

A second aspect of human evil to which we might point is called the post-traumatic stress disorder, PTSD for short. In many ways it is opposite to human sacrifice and to the enjoyment of horror films and stories. Only now, in the last two decades, is this psychological phenomenon being identified. Only in our time is it being dealt with. Today, as never before in human history, we are beginning to comprehend the desolating impact of human evil, not only on its intended victims, but upon those who witness it.

The trauma suffered by so many of the veterans of the Vietnam War, that of the survivors of the Holocaust in Nazi Germany, together with recent revelations of domestic violence—incest in particular—have shown us that the witness, no less than the victim, can be traumatized by iniquity too terrifying to recall. We turn such experiences in upon ourselves, it seems, burying them so deep inside us we do not know they are there. Yet those memories live on, unseen, unknown to the conscious mind, gnawing at us, twisting the psyche into patterns of abnormal behavior, and all too often, destroying us in the end.

Do you doubt what I write? If it has been your good fortune to have enjoyed a somewhat protected life, you owe it to yourself to read a book such as N. Duncan Sinclair's *Horrific Traumata: A Pastoral Response to the Post-Traumatic Stress Disorder*.[6] In a brief, stunningly vivid one hundred pages the author relates at firsthand stories of people he has known in all walks of life who have been traumatized by human evil, either as victims or as witnesses, or both.

In excruciating detail, Sinclair sets examples of great trauma before the reader and explains how they work. Himself a Vietnam veteran and chaplain who had been traumatized, Sinclair explains the destructive impact of the war upon sensitive young men. He does the same with stories from civilian life. His book and others like it fill us with despair.

And yet, as we sweat out the harrowing tales these writers recount in an attempt to deal with PTSD, we begin to sense an unexpected stirring of hope within us. We are struck by the power of evil to destroy the psyche of the innocent. But if this be so, we find ourselves wondering, does there lie in such traumas hope for humanity? I think there does, and in two quite different respects. First and most obviously there now is hope for the victims of PTSD. Having identified this heretofore elusive phenomenon, we can begin to break its hold upon its victims. Apparently we are now learning to do just that.

But secondly and far more importantly, in identifying PTSD and learning how to deal with it, we have learned something about ourselves we humans badly need to know. There is hope for a creature who, not having known blood and gore, killing, rape, and incest, can be traumatized by confronting such experiences. Ours is not a false hope rising out of a revulsion from evil. It is an assessment of human nature. If the innocent can be disabled by human suffering, there is hope for us all. Deep within us apparently lies the potential for a genuine empathy for one another. In that fact, if indeed it is a fact, lies a very great hope for humanity in the long, if not in the short term.

But let us not rejoice too soon. There is no justice here. The evil we do to one another destroys the innocent, not the guilty. It is the good, not the wicked, who are traumatized. The good suffer because they are good. They are traumatized because they cannot abide crass human evil and are powerless to prevent it. But hope lies with a creature like that. Hope lies with us humans if we can be so sickened by gross and needless injury to others that we ourselves are destroyed by it. Hope lies with a creature who can care that much for others.

We have, then, to see to our surroundings. We have to provide an environment for our children, not one in which they grow insensitive to pain, but one in which violence brings pain to the body and soul of those who behold it.

Moral Principles Can Grow

In the new paradigm for religion moral principles are little different from those that prevail in religion generally, but with a conspicuous exception. The new paradigm for religion rejects outright the commonly accepted notion of eternal principles of right and wrong. The problem here for the inquiring mind is a part of its larger problem with traditional theology. The best code that can be devised is eventually outgrown. In the course of time understanding broadens and deepens. What once seemed to be eternally right no longer seems so in a new cultural context. Perhaps one day we humans shall achieve the empathy which is now such a high and seemingly unattainable goal for us all. That day may be long in coming. Then again, it may come soon. For the open mind and the open heart, our task is to keep the impossible dream ever before us, and to move resolutely toward it with all the speed we can command.

If we turn back to the ancient Greeks, we find that they believed life consists in "a harmonious culmination of human potentialities."[7] Translated from philosophical jargon, that means we humans are engaged in a process of personal and social observation and discovery, whereby we learn at firsthand what does and what does not make for what we perceive the good life to be. Moral principles are worked out in practice. We formulate them and modify them as we observe the degree to which they make possible the good life for all.

Forgiveness

Here is another example of the evolution of moral principles. The forgiveness of God has been central in the ethics of Christianity since New Testament times. A beloved old Gospel hymn begins:

If I have wounded any soul today
If I have caused one foot to go astray
If I have wandered in my willful way
Dear Lord, forgive.

This hymn has troubled me for as long as I can remember. It starts out fine with the concern we ought all to feel for one another. The third line throws us off a little. What does it really mean? Willful against whom, for what? But the final line of the verse destroys the hymn for anyone who feels at home in the new paradigm for religion. At least it does for me, and I suspect I am not alone.

The inquirer would ask: In what sense is it a virtue to seek the forgiveness of God, whom we don't know, when we have hurt a creature of earth, whom we do? The religions traditionally have stressed our need of divine forgiveness for wrongdoing. Atonement, expiation, sacrifice, and penitence have been called for. The emphasis has been on human sin as an offense to the deity. In the new paradigm for religion the emphasis shifts from the divine to the human; from a transgression of divine law to the suffering of a fellow human whose pain we have caused. Whether or not divine law was offended is left to the theologians to debate.

In the new paradigm for religion virtue does not consist in piety toward some far-off deity. It consists in a pattern of conduct that gives to other people the respect and the love we ourselves yearn for. The virtuous person is the one who is drawn to others in need. True virtue requires that we mend any hurt we may cause anyone, whether intentional or unintentional. True virtue requires that we follow the path of righteousness because we care about other people. That is what righteousness is. When we have been so foolish or malicious as to have hurt someone, we may beg divine forgiveness if we wish, but our first duty is to right the wrong we have done to the best of our ability. The Good Samaritan, not the penitent, is the model of those whose standard is that of the open mind and heart in religion.

In the religion of the open mind and heart forgiveness enters the picture when we ourselves have been hurt. We can attain no higher ideal than the capacity to forgive when we have been intentionally harmed. To do so requires a profound understanding of human character, and beyond that, a charity of spirit few of us can boast. Really to forgive an intentional affront or deprivation or injury is to achieve a high degree of empathy. It is to see that there lurks in the best of us the primitive instincts of the predator. Always we are beset by the impulse to gain for ourselves at the expense of others. In the lower reaches of some of us a perverse desire to hurt others for our own pleasure may arise. Yet a true empathy for our fellow creatures may arise at the same time and overcome the lower, more primitive impulse. A true empathy remains the goal, ever glowing before us all.

The Impossible Ideal

The Golden Rule is the formula, stated concisely. But be not deceived. Carried all the way, made to apply to everything we do, it is impossible to follow. Most of us don't come close. Try as we may, we are simply incapable of always doing for every other person what, if put in their shoes, we might wish they would do for us. All too many of us make this an excuse for throwing up our hands and ceasing to try at all. So we call for a scaled down practical set of principles to follow, a kind of Silver Rule that gives us some chance of succeeding to replace the Golden standard that forever condemns us to failure.

There is another problem with the Golden Rule as a simple and practical guide for living. Great moral principles are easily stated. They are grand to behold. But they can be held to completely only when we are operating with people whose actions are guided by similar principles. If not—if we find we are dealing with people waiting to take advantage of us—the rules change. Unless we are aware of the plotting of such people and take precautions against them, our nobility becomes stupidity and our would-be high morality is reduced to folly.

To this very real problem, those who hold to the new paradigm for religion respond: Life, as we are given it to live, is always a compromise. At every point, we must compromise between the ideal and the practical, the dream and the reality, the hoped for and the doable. In all things, ethics and morality included, we can only do what we can. That is where we are in life, not only in ethics, but in politics and economics, athletics, astrophysics, and art. We cannot jump over the moon. Neither can we always in every instance live by the Golden Rule.

Nevertheless, in the new paradigm for religion we begin by insisting that the goal of doing so to the best of our ability remains ever implacably before us. It is irreplaceable and inescapable. Practical limitations do not release us from the demand the moral ideal lays upon us. Truly moral people must always strive for perfection that they know they cannot attain. Always they must strive on, mending their ways as best they can, righting their errors and their wrongs as best they can, never deterred by the fact that the goal for which they strive is beyond their reach. In the new paradigm for religion we learn to live with our fallibility and our moral lapses as well. But we also learn never to tolerate in ourselves or in anyone else a pattern of wrongdoing in which our gain is someone else's hurt, or any relaxing of our determination to follow the moral imperative as far as we can.

Human Society

Truly moral behavior is difficult to achieve among other reasons because moral principles are so pervasive. Like waves set up in the water, moral principles, once formulated and applied, just go on and on. For example, our personal mores, the code of conduct in accordance with which we deal with other people, is only the beginning. An appreciation of the needs of others when it is realistic quickly moves from the personal to the societal. Social structures are central with us humans. Moral precepts make our social structures necessary. They also make society possible.

In the new paradigm for religion democracy is the central principle of organization for a truly moral social structure. It grows out of concern for the welfare of the individual. People are the units out of which democracies are built. In a moral society, one that encourages in its citizens a striving for the Golden Rule, the needs of others always take their place, not ahead of, not behind, but alongside of one's own.

The subject of democracy, like many of the others germain to this inquiry, needs no elaboration here. It will be enough to illustrate the way the Golden Rule works within structures that are democratic in substance as well as form. To do so, let us turn to little democracies—voluntary associations they are called, sometimes mediating structures. I choose them as an example because it is an area of activity I have known at firsthand throughout my life.

In my profession as a minister in a democratically organized church (Unitarian Universalist) I first learned how well small democratic structures can work to achieve their goals and at the same time to benefit their members. The Unitarian Universalists, ever the stout defenders of creedlessness, of open inquiry and open debate, always strive for the full participation of all hands both in discussion and in the action that supposedly follows. Outside the denomination, as an urban minister and community activist, I participated in a number of nonecclesiastical "good will" organizations, boards, commissions, and committees. Nearly all of them were also voluntary associations, genuinely democratic in structure and in the way they functioned in practice.

In retirement, with an avocation in forestry and environmental affairs, I see once more how effectively, if not always perfectly, little democracies achieve high social goals and develop human character, thought, and purpose, all at the same time. On boards, commissions, and committees at the local, state, and national level, under widely varying circumstances, I again see at firsthand and participate in a variety of little democracies, different from those I had known in the church and in civic affairs, yet remarkably similar to them. As with the other groups, some of the forestry and environmental organizations function with a salaried executive at the head, supported by a paid staff, and often a huge number of volunteers. Many others are entirely volunteer in their makeup. But all alike are concerned with human welfare, or are supposed to be, and all strive to achieve the democratic ideal of full participation of each of the members, on an equal basis for everyone. Not all do so, to be sure, but most do.

Entering the field of environmental concerns, focused on forestry, I am struck by the similarity of human types that make up the boards and committees on which I work. They exhibit the same mix of competence and incompetence, dedication and vainglory, industry and indolence I had known before. All alike require infinite patience with compulsive talkers and with those who are eager to hold office, yet who accomplish little, clinging to the office they hold while the work they should have been doing remains undone. On the other hand, all I find offer to true believers who want nothing more than to serve humanity in its manifold needs, an opportunity to give of themselves, their time, and such talent as they have to something really worthwhile.

Alexis de Tocqueville

It was Alexis de Tocqueville who first noted the widespread development of voluntary associations in the United States. He might or might not be surprised to see the extent to which the movement has since grown in this country and the number and variety of self-organized, self-governing "little democracies" thriving in the American body politic today, a hundred and fifty years after his time.

The late James Luther Adams of the Harvard Divinity School, ministerial colleague and lifelong friend, stands at the forefront of a group of scholars who, for a generation or more, have been insisting on the importance of little democracies in American life today. A festschrift on the subject was published in Adams's honor in 1966. Penetrating to the basics of voluntary associations, Adams points to their dual role: (1) their ability to achieve their published goals, and (2) their ability to provide an environment that fosters the growth of the individual participant. Each of the members of a small but genuinely democratic structure learns through participation in the group to develop, to propose and then to defend his or her own ideas, and to enjoy the sense of gratification and achievement when the group takes seriously what they say.

Most of us are aware of the power and usefulness of such groups in bringing about social reform. The labor movement, the women's movement, the civil rights movement, and the peace movement are cases in point. So, too, are the innumerable schools, libraries, hospitals, and social service agencies that have been organized, financed, and operated by self-organized and self-governed citizen associations. We have seen it also in the setting up of foundations dedicated to meeting social needs of all kinds, some trivial, many of great and lasting importance.

The Environmental Movement

The flowering of the environmental movement in the United States and increasingly worldwide in the last three decades of the twentieth century is currently demonstrating the way in which little democracies can powerfully influence public policy. We have only to cite the success of organizations like the Nature Conservancy, the Audubon Society, the Sierra Club, the Natural Resources Defense Council, the Wilderness Society, and the astonishing growth of the Land Trust movement within the last ten years. Today, for the first time in history, people are coming to understand that concern for other people means concern for the small planet on which we find ourselves living. Today, at last, we are beginning to see that Earth itself is as important as the people who live upon it.

Earth, too, must now be included on the list of things demanding self-restraint on the part of anyone with any pretense to virtue. If morality is measured by the harm we do to others, as the new paradigm for religion insists, the new Great Commandment is that we restrain our self-indulgence planet-wide. We must now begin to measure everything we do by its impact upon our little planet in its totality. Earth is our home. Without it we cannot exist. What the future holds we do not know. For now we know that the health of our planet and our health are one. It will be so for our children. They will inherit what we leave behind. What sort of homeland are we preparing for them, for their children, and for their children's children? We can ask no more important question than that.

The Future

There is no doubt in my mind that the vitality of the United States today is due in no small part to its voluntary associations. It is quite possible, however, that the twentieth century will have seen the high water mark of the voluntary association movement in America. Too many such groups today have learned how to disrupt a peaceful society as a means to their own private and not always noble ends. Too many, nowadays, seem to be willing to go to almost any length to force their particular agenda on society as a whole. Their goal is no longer to bring their case before the body politic and persuade people of its validity. Their goal, high-minded though it may have been at the outset, is no longer to achieve assent. It has become victory, by persuasion if possible, and if not, by any means necessary. In high self-righteousness they resort to disruption so intolerable that a helpless body politic gives in to their demands.

Ironically, it is the institutions of freedom that make these evils possible. Indeed, human woe often is due to the subversion of laws designed to help the helpless. Free societies build a great variety of structures to improve the status of their citizens, the voluntary association being conspicuous among them. But they are easily subverted by the avaricious. All too often they are.

The Moral Imperative

To attempt more than an example or two of specific moral principles and the way they work in practice is impossible in an inquiry that attempts to outline so broad a concept as a new paradigm for religion. Perhaps the foregoing will serve our purposes. Truly moral behavior rises from within us, not from high-minded social structures or from high-minded laws of the state enforced by the police and the courts. Moral principles are observed for their own sake, voluntarily, by people who think it is important to do so. Moral principles are followed voluntarily and gladly by a truly moral person. Such a person recognizes the needs and desires, the hopes and anxieties of other people. A truly moral person is motivated neither by the fear of being caught nor by the hope of social acclaim. In contemporary terminology, a moral person is inner-directed. Other-directed people guide their lives by the prevailing attitudes and practices of their place and time. They are guided by externals. Inner-directed people are guided by a clearly formulated self-consistent system of moral principles in which they themselves deeply believe, and which they follow as best they can.

Perhaps it is enough to conclude by saying that in the new paradigm for religion all moral principles arise from the single fact that we are not alone, you and I, the hermit in the desert no more than someone living at the center of a huge metropolis like Mexico City. We need one another personally. But we are bound no less to respect one another. We are bound to one another by virtue of being what we are, human creatures. But within this bond lies the self-restraint that holds us back from imposing on one another. And so we say: Whatever we would ask of others for ourselves, we must in conscience grant to them when they ask it of us.

Would you call for help in time of need? Then stand ready to help when others call to you for help. Would you ask for food when you are hungry? Then feed the hungry when they turn to you. Would you be loved by those around you? Then offer them your love without stint, without expecting or seeking repayment, yet accepting love gladly and with gratitude when it comes to you. In the new paradigm for religion we find ourselves with great personal needs to fill. So do all people. As we seek help in filling our needs, so we help others in filling theirs.

This is the moral imperative, compelling and inescapable. It is well named the Golden Rule. No deity in any heaven could lay a heavier burden upon us. Nor could any deity reward us more fully than we are rewarded when we come as close to that ideal as we can.

The Faith of the New Paradigm for Religion

Have we now achieved the elusive goal of this inquiry? Have we been able to cast into language the basic beliefs of those who reject the old paradigm of belief by faith through revelation? Have we been able to state the beliefs that emerge when we have thought them through as far as an open mind and heart and spirit can? Let the reader judge. It is a basic canon of the new paradigm that in the end it is we—you and I—who decide.

As we strive to formulate a life philosophy or personal credo or set of basic beliefs, it steadily becomes clear that the undertaking can have no end. The results we achieve, whatever they may be, cannot be compressed into a small well-wrought code. An attempt to state the faith of the new paradigm ends, not in a carefully crafted document, but in something more like a tapestry—not a static weaving of multicolored threads, but an ever-changing kaleidoscope of color, like a New England hillside in autumn.

There is drama beyond compare in such a scene. In our family, we see it annually across the fields to the west of our home in the hills of western Maine. There, at first unaware that we were doing so, we built what we now call our autumn garden. Years ago we noticed that the same trees turned the same brilliant color each year. Haphazardly at first, then systematically, we began cutting away the less colorful stems to allow the more brilliant ones room to grow. The result is a stunning display each year of red and gold beyond the green fields, backed by a clear blue or dark beclouded sky.

A personal belief structure is like that for the inquirer in religion. It is a great mix of ever-changing, often brilliant, sometimes dismal thoughts and ideas. As the colors on a forested hillside change from day to day, so, too, do the concepts in our idea-patterns. The details grow and diminish, come on and fade even as we watch them. As the forest itself is the constant in an autumn scene so the pattern of religious ideas that are ours remains, while the details in it wax and wane.

Does the life philosophy of the inquirer disintegrate in the end, as autumn leaves eventually shrivel and fall? Here the analogy breaks down as analogies, pressed too far, will do. Inquirers find, on the contrary, that a well thought out belief system lives and grows. The multivaried elements in it may change, and the emphasis may shift as the circumstances of life draw one or another of the principles to the fore. But the whole remains even as the forest remains, when the last leaf of summer has fallen to the ground.

The Liberal faith is like any other. If it is well conceived, well founded, and well thought out, it will guide and sustain us through the trials of life. In fact, it is at this point, where the Liberal faith is said to be weakest, that we find its greatest strength. A faith in which the unrelenting pursuit of truth and right is never compromised and never given up—the Liberal faith—came into existence because of the inability of the traditional faiths to provide a belief structure that could adapt itself to the growing idea structure of the culture of which it was a part, and so compel the allegiance of an open mind and heart. This the Liberal faith strives to do. Its goal is a pattern of belief that compels believing because it satisfies a heart that aspires to the highest reaches of morality, a mind that aspires to cosmic understanding, and a spirit that never rests as it reaches toward the infinite and eternal—toward what we mean by the "Divine" when we are the best of what we mean by "human."

Notes

1. Matthew 7:12.

2. Arnold S. Relman, "Fraud in Science: Causes and Remedies," *Scientific American* (April 1989): 126.

3. Scott Degarmo, "The Art of Deception," Editor's note, *Success* (March 1994): 4.

4. Vachel Lindsay, "Johnny Appleseed's Hymn" from *Collected Works* (Macmillan Company, 1925).

5. William Blake, "Milton" in *Romantic Poets*, ed. W. H. Auden (New York: The Viking Press, 1950), p. 24.

6. N. Duncan Sinclair, *Horrific Traumata: A Pastoral Response to the Post-Traumatic Stress Disorder* (New York: Haworth Pastoral Press, 1993).

7. Bernard Williams, *Ethics and the Limits of Philosophy* (Cambridge, Mass.: Harvard University Press, 1985).

Part Four

The Ultimate Question

In Part Three we developed four basic articles of faith that emerge when we follow the testing, questing process as far as it will go, never resting until no questions are left to ask and no further concepts can be formulated. What more can we say? We might begin to spell out the details that are implied in the four principles we have formulated and the knowledge and understanding they involve, until we have written an encyclopedia. More to our purpose, we can arbitrarily stop here with the ultimate question toward which this inquiry has been pointing: What is the meaning and purpose of life? How may we best determine what it is?

The answer to these questions is not to be found here or anywhere else. It carries within itself an assumption, the error in which we are only now, in our time, really beginning to see. Ever since we humans first achieved self-consciousness, we have sought eternal Truth, known, it was supposed, only to the gods. Today we are beginning to see that our human condition does not yield final answers to ultimate questions.

Now, in our time, we are moving from a God-centered, church-centered, Bible-centered faith to one that is human-centered. Today our faith is based on the principles of testing, questing, and never resting in our pursuit of truth. We are moving from authority to inquiry, from dogma to discovery, from beliefs given to us by a church to the continuous reformulation of whatever faith is more persuasive to us. We are moving from hope for eternal bliss in the next world to mending our ways in this one. Awe, wonder, and a sense of ever-deepening mystery are not lessened in the process, they are increased. So, too, are the problems. But so, too, are the joys and satisfactions our religion brings to us. All are a part of what it means for you and me—each of us individually and all of us taken together—to find ourselves alive, wondering why this is so, what we are to think, and what we ought to do.

18

Life's Meaning and Purpose

The infinite and the eternal are always present. Our question is what we are going to do about them. How are we to think of ourselves in the presence of the infinite and eternal? So tiny and so transient, one among billions, how can I count for anything? My life span is but a flick in the passing of time. How can anything I say or do or think matter at all?

As with so many of the issues with which we have dealt, to ask about the meaning and purpose of life is to make an important assumption. Maybe life doesn't have any real meaning, or any true purpose. Down through the centuries, more than one great thinker has concluded that the question must, in all honesty, be answered in the negative. As we have already noted, Pyrrho of Elis, back in the third century B.C.E., was among the first to follow the process of inquiry consistently as far as it would go. He ended in ultimate skepticism, we recall, uncertain of everything, and with neither guidance nor much hope for living. In our own time, Bertrand Russell did the same. As a young man the British philosopher wrote an essay entitled "The Free Man's Worship," now the classic statement of the cosmic despair to which strict reasoning can bring one. Russell concluded:

"The life of man is a long march through the night, surrounded by invisible foes, tortured by weariness and pain, toward a goal that few can hope to reach, and where none may tarry long. One by one as they march, our comrades vanish from our sight, seized by the silent orders of omnipotent death. . . . Brief and powerless is man's life; on him and all his race the slow sure doom falls pitiless and dark. Blind to good and evil, reckless of destruction, omnipotent matter rolls on its relentless way. Man condemned today to lose his dearest, tomorrow himself to pass through the gate of darkness, [nevertheless] preserves a mind free from the wanton tyranny that rules his outward life . . . , proudly defiant to sustain alone the world his own ideals have fashioned despite the trampling march of unconscious power."[1]

Contemporary writers have repeated the refrain although with less poetic flair. Steven Weinberg (*The First Three Minutes*, 1977) wrote: "The more the universe seems comprehensible the more it also seems pointless."[2] James Trefil (*The Dark Side of the Universe*, 1988) wrote: "No matter what the composition of the universe, the end will be the same—a cold expanding sea of radiation, from which all life has long since vanished."[3]

Great Metaphysical Schemes

By no means, however, have all philosophers felt themselves driven to such a conclusion. Quite the opposite. By equally strict reasoning the large majority have attempted, and in the eyes of most people, have succeeded in finding meaning in life—Plato and Aristotle among the ancients; Spinoza, Descartes, Kant, Hegel, and Whitehead more recently. But we look long and hard for agreement among them. Today the debate still goes on as to what the basics of life and thought, experience and existence really are.

For vast numbers of people, of course, there is no problem. They stay happily in the religious tradition in which they grew up, where the answers to life's most basic questions are solid, clear, and persuasive as well. The traditional religions have evolved their answers over long periods of time. For centuries their teachings have been tested, elaborated, explained, and defended against all the doubts and questions that could be flung at them.

What of the new paradigm for religion? There the answers to life's basic questions are only beginning to take shape. Those who find the new paradigm congenial are a mix. Some turn to philosophy for formulas that best express their thinking. Some turn to science, some to literature, poetry, or drama. Most turn to them all in varying degrees according to their personal tastes and needs. Many people come up with answers that are very much alike. Others vary greatly from one to another in their views. Many more people of an open mind and heart in religion simply do not think much about these things one way or the other. They are too busy—until a calamity befalls them. Then they, too, begin wondering what it means to be alive, to know joy, when sorrow suddenly overwhelms them; to know exultation, and see it devastated in misery, anxiety, and pain.

Here again, no small part of the problem is a false assumption hidden in the question we are asking. Speculating on the meaning of life, we assume without realizing it that the answer will be found in a great over-arching, all-encompassing philosophy like that of Plato or Aristotle, Kant or Hegel. In religion we are apt to assume that the answer will be found in a great theological construct like that of Augustine or Thomas Aquinas, together with the modifications, additions, and corrections of, say, Martin Luther, John Calvin, Karl Barth, or Paul Tillich.

We are easily misled by the seeming success of the towering edifices of the human mind and spirit descending to us from earlier times. But we need to ask whether a continuing succession of masterworks is the route we ought to take. As their authors have conceded, none of the systems the human mind has worked out have proved to be final. At best they turn out to be building blocks only in our continuing attempt to answer life's most basic questions. We are heirs to a succession of truly great theologies and philosophies developed by the great minds of the ages. They demonstrate the capacity of the human mind for extraordinary feats of thinking and of inspiration. But what we humans have done with those systems, in particular when they have been adopted as the official position of an ecclesiastical institution, is appalling. A bloodstained history shows how far we can be misled when in religion we sanctify the thinking of an earlier day.

We should know by now that the meaning of life will not be found in a yet greater metaphysical or theological scheme. From Genesis to Aristotle to Wittgenstein, the thought of great minds has too often become a prison house for later generations. Great philosophies and theologies are intended to liberate, but they can do so only if we think of them not as final truth in any sense but only as formulations upon which we build better structures tomorrow.

Many have supposed that science will one day be able to answer all our questions. But if we begin with the present day speculation about the Big Bang and with the final result of that colossal event billions of years hence, where does that take us? Go to the books of cosmology or philosophy if that is your wish. You will not find life's meaning and purpose there. Go to the books of theology. You will not find the answer there either. The sacred literature of the world will help you more, but too much of it was written in an earlier time in a mental framework too strange for those books alone to give us the help we need today.

Awe, Wonder, and Mystery

In the new paradigm for religion we begin in the here and now. We look about us, see what we can see, read everything we can find; we immerse ourselves in the wisdom of the ages. From it all we draw the conclusions toward which the entire corpus seems to point.

Following such a course we find ourselves asking: What is beautiful? How do we know it is beautiful? What is ugly? How do we know that something is ugly? What is enjoyable? What is harmful? What is noble? What is low and mean? We can go on asking, but where are the answers? What is true? What is good, in the natural world and in the human world? Frustrated, we change and begin asking why. Why do the true, the beautiful, and the good seem so important to us? How are we to account for the love that flows out from us and back to us, and so often overwhelms us? How can we achieve these wonders and glories in our own lives? That is what we really care about.

Striving to see our world, not as we might wish it were, but as it really is, we find that, in the end, mystery surrounds us on every side. As the religions have always said, in the end we come to the unknown—not the unknowable but to mystery which we continually strive to penetrate.

The problem with traditional religion for the Liberal is its claim to have got to the heart of Mystery through divine revelation. Often the word is capitalized as if to endow it with divinity by verbal sleight of hand. "Mystery," the traditionalists say, is known by faith. Inquirers counter that no such theological shortcut is available to us. Mystery is not a place; it is a process. We are continually moving into the unknown, but we are not there yet. We see no prospect of attaining full knowledge at any time in the forseeable future. Meanwhile, we look upon whatever lies beyond us as exactly that. It is what lies beyond us. It is not shrinking. Daily it grows wider, deeper, and yet more mysterious.

What the ancients identified as Deity and many today call "Mystery" is where any theology comes out. So, too, does the theology or metaphysics or philosophy of the true Liberal in religion. Despite all the accusations of secularism, unbelief, even atheism flung against them, inquirers are the first, not the last, to acknowledge with all religious people that the questioning process concludes not with the certainty we yearn for but in awe and wonder—in mystery that invites us ever into its all-enveloping totality.

In the new paradigm for religion all people of all shades and varieties of opinion are seen to be at one with one another in the sense of awe and wonder our world evokes in us. When we humans gaze up at the stars at night, they speak to us of infinity and eternity without our really understanding what those terms mean. They have ever since we first developed the capacity to wonder at what we beheld and tried to find meaning in it. When we built telescopes and turned them upon those same stars, they began speaking to us with a clearer voice, because we were able to understand a little better what they really are. When we turned our radioscopes upon stardust clouds that obscured our vision and were able to penetrate them, the heavens have spoken to us more clearly still.

As we learned, as we accumulated more and more knowledge and understanding about what we saw, and as we achieved a clearer understanding of what it meant, our sense of astonishment did not lessen, it increased. As we began to piece together the story of how our universe originated, as if we had been there to see it billions of years ago—*billions*—then our throats have gone dry, our eyes have glazed over, and an ecstasy has seized us as the incredible nature of it all took form in our conscious minds.

We humans have already gathered an unbelievable amount of knowledge and understanding. We have done so in an unbelievably short space of time, measuring time by the age of the universe. Virtually all of what we know has come to us within the last four or five thousand years. Most of it has come within the last few centuries, the bulk of this within the lifetime of many of us. Who shall say how much more there is to learn? Who would dare guess? Does it matter that we do not, perhaps cannot, know? Is it not enough that we are on our way?

The New Paradigm for Religion

In the new paradigm for religion, more and more it becomes clear that life's meaning and purpose will not be found where we have been looking for it. The answer to life's final question does not reside in a super thought-pattern of philosophical speculation, nor is it to be found in a revelation from on high transcending all knowledge and all thought. The answer to life's final question does not reside in a structure we humans have pieced together, whether scientific or philosphical or theological. It is found in the structuring. It will not be found in an edifice of thought we have built, but in the building of it. We shall never arrive at the final thought structure so many seek. We shall always be building, always inventing new and better ones. Therein lies the joy, the exultation, the worth of living. It is not in the being, but in the doing; not in a cathedral of thought so perfect we fall upon our knees before it, but in the ongoing process of discovery, overwhelming because of the new knowledge and understanding it continually pours upon us.

In the new paradigm for religion life's meaning and purpose are found where religion has always found it, in ourselves. Knowledge may seem to come from the skies as we gaze into the firmament and thrill at what we see. Yes, that is what we see. But it is we who do the seeing. It is we who find meaning in what we see. It is we, you and I, who are filled with awe and wonder at it all. It is we who find a sense of the spiritual rising within us as we contemplate the immensity of what we behold.

Continual, purposeful seeking in religion shifts the focus of the experience, and the way we understand and interpret it. For the traditionalists our understanding is derived from ancient documents, rituals, traditions, institutions, and practices. For the inquirer our understanding is derived from the present. That present includes all that the past has shown us. But it includes yet more: an open mind and an open heart in all of their teeming dimensions, supremely in religion, as we address the here and now.

Basics

Perhaps the most basic article of faith in the new paradigm for religion is our confidence that we humans can succeed at the task life sets for us, even if only in part. In chapter 14 we spoke of the conviction that rises unbidden within us that we have the capacity to grow in knowledge and understanding, and that through such a religion we can begin to grasp the meaning of life. It tells us that we can do it better by looking to the present and the future than by looking to the past alone. But we can do it only by testing the judgments we make, not against ancient dogma, but against the clearest thinking of which we are capable in the here and now; only by questing for ever wider, deeper, and more accurate knowledge and under-standing, and only by never resting as we pursue these goals.

If we start there; if we hold stubbornly and unflinchingly to the goal of drawing up the best set of basic beliefs we can contrive, and if we keep fluid the result to which we are brought, we are confident that everything else will fall in place. That is what I have attempted here. It is doubtless why in the writing of this book the material on the believing *process* kept growing, while the concluding section, which was to have been a full statement of the faith of the new paradigm for religion, either frayed off and shrank, or conversely seemed to require to be expanded without limit, forever.

Where the Logic of Liberalism Leads

If we follow the logic of Liberalism, which means following it all the way to the end, and if we then take the new paradigm for religion as our own, a final question rises to haunt us. Does not the fatal flaw we find at the heart of Liberalism lie at the heart of all religion? In particular, is it not a major problem for anyone whose basic thought structure is that of the Western intellectual tradition? Like the Liberals today's traditionalists also live their "secular" lives by the tenets and standards that evolved in the universities of the West. They, too, participate in and enjoy the achievements of science and of the scientific method.

If a basic inner contradiction could bring down Liberalism in a few short years, could not that same inner contradiction eventually bring down the great established religions of the West as well? If the fatal flaw in Liberalism was that it attempted the impossible, may it not be that the same flaw is eating at the heart of mainline religion in the West today? Would the religious idealism which once was real in the West become real again if the Western intellectual tradition and the Western religious tradition were to become one?

Western culture today faces a profound problem it has yet to address openly. Why are its scientific accomplishments so astonishing while its social problems continue to mount? Why is there such widespread skepticism among the mainline religions while only the fanatics' and believers' lives are really governed by their religion?

Those who have found in the new paradigm for religion an answer to their own religious problems cannot but ask: Might not the West, and perhaps the world as well, move toward solving the giant social problems that plague us today if they, too, were to adopt the new paradigm for religion? Would not a consistent pattern of thought, uniting religious, social, scientific, and practical concerns worldwide serve us better than the present division between Truth in religion known by revelation, and truth that all of us share, slowly pieced together according to Western standards of thought?

We shall have religion, you and I, whether we want it or not. Like breathing and thinking and loving, religion is a part of us. As the thoroughgoing Liberals see it, our question is not whether we are to have religion but what kind of religion we are to have. This question, and the burning desire to answer it with a religion that lifts us to the highest degree we know, and is believed in the deepest parts of our being, provides the motive power for true Liberalism.

Since we humans came down from the trees and emerged from the jungle, our religion has provided much-needed social cohesion and social control. It still can, but only if we really honor its practices and genuinely believe its teachings. While increasing turmoil besets the free societies of the West today, the cohesion and control formerly provided by the religions disintegrates. Is there not a connection between these two alarming phenomena? If there is, should we not seek out and implement a religion pitched at the highest moral and spiritual level but also one that is thoroughly believable and therefore thoroughly persuasive to most people?

The battles that have raged between religious sects and groups since ancient times have been power struggles. That is clear. What has not been so clear is that these battles reveal our innate sense of the importance of religious faith. As we have seen in the course of this inquiry, the beliefs of the religion we embrace determine our basic mindset. Our religious faith tells us who we are, what we should do, and why. The way we think determines what we do, and that in turn very largely determines what others can and cannot do in their dealings with us. People with high moral principles, and with self-control to match, make life easy and beautiful for us. People who believe themselves to be superior, and therefore privileged, can make life a nightmare for everyone but themselves.

We humans can destroy ourselves through the avarice of a few, their actions made possible by the thoughtlessness of the many. We can destroy the planet in a nuclear holocaust or decimate it with pollution and overpopulation. But with our minds we can foresee these dangers and design remedies to meet them. We can let our religion become irrelevant, providing us with comfort based only on hope. We can let it become ineffective through neglect. We can allow our religion to become pernicious through fanaticism. But we can also face the problems life sets before us, think them all the way through and solve them by providing humanity with a religion that is believed because it is persuasive. Such a religion will move us to act because it is believed, not because it is said to be divine, but because its validity has been tested to the uttermost.

Is there then nothing that is set apart? Is there nothing sacred rather than secular, nothing genuinely holy? In the new paradigm for religion, everything is a unity. But within that unity there are qualitative differences. Some are so great that they amount to a difference in kind. The beauty/ugliness contrast is an example. Most things are a mix, but at either end of the scale few of us have trouble deciding what is beautiful and what is ugly. So it is with all things.

In the new paradigm for religion our universe is a *uni*verse, because, at least for now, there is no clear evidence that we should base our thinking on any other premise.

We End Where We Began

At this point we conclude, not because we have reached the end of our inquiry, for we have not. We have scarcely begun. We conclude because life's meaning and purpose and the best means of finding it are not to be perceived by one person or a thousand or ten million. Neither can it be written out and established by the greatest council we might gather. Ultimate meanings are always in the process of being formulated as all of us together do our best to lay hold of some corner of Reality and try to convey to everyone else what we have found.

We end where we began, as inquirers, as seekers. But we end with a clearer concept of the task before us. We do not end with a bigger, better, more satisfying philosophical or theological system. We end by calling for a new understanding of what religion itself is at its best.

We have already learned a lot, but it is clear that we still have an infinite way to go on the path to truth. We shall continue to learn only if we cease thinking of ourselves as God's chosen beings, a little lower than the angels. We shall end in folly and disaster, destruction, despair, and death unless we face up to the reality of our human condition. We are fallible creatures in all things, including religion. Our supposed knowledge is fallible, including religious knowledge, even the part the religions regard as divine in origin. Religion enjoys no private avenue to Truth. The old paradigm has no answer for fanatics who claim to have the Truth, delivered to them by God. In the new paradigm for religion fanaticism is impossible.

Sunlight

Plato is generally conceded to have been one of the greatest minds we humans have produced. Nevertheless in Book VII of the *Republic* he resorted to a very simple metaphor in order to explain his concept of the knowledge we humans possess and the understanding of it we have achieved. Plato elaborated his metaphor at great length, but the central point any child could grasp.

Imagine, he wrote, a group of men chained in a dark cave. They can see nothing but shadows cast on the wall before them by figures passing in front of a fire they also cannot see. If one of the prisoners were released, Plato continues, and could at last see the figures, only the shadows of which he had been able to see heretofore, would he not find it difficult to relate them to those shadows? Suppose, Plato went on, the prisoner was then dragged out into the sunlight. Would he not be dazzled by the light, and unable for a time to see much of anything? Ultimately, however, his eyes would adjust and he would be able to see like the rest of us.

Plato's metaphor, as he develops it, is much more subtle and complex, interwoven with his philosophy of Forms, of Goodness and Reality, into which we need not go. Scholars think that his imagery was derived from the rituals of Greek religion held in caves that symbolically represented the underworld. The candidates for initiation into the Greek mystery religions often were led from such dark places into the presence of sacred objects flooded with light. Plato's main point, however, is simple and plain. We humans, with our limited capacities, are like men chained in a cave watching shadows.

I beg leave to follow Plato's example with a metaphor drawn from our own time, containing elements more familiar to us than those of a cave where the Greek Orphic mysteries were celebrated. Consider instead an old farmhouse on a ridge in the foothills of the White Mountains in New England. I can speak of it at firsthand, because it is in such a place that I now live.

On cool clear autumn days we often wake in the morning to find ourselves in the midst of a fog so thick you can see almost nothing out the windows. Then slowly, imperceptibly, something almost magical begins to happen. As the sun climbs higher in the sky, the mist begins to thin out. First the shrubs outside the window appear, then a bit of the lawn around the house. Next ghostly shadows of the shade trees begin to take form. Then the barn looms out of the mist like a great ship bearing down on us. The stone walls across the fields emerge, followed by the first faint outline of the trees in the forest beyond. Then range after range of the hills in the distance take their accustomed places, and finally the mountains on the horizon. Above it all the sky becomes a glistening blue, and our world is flooded with sunlight.

Nature's drama, played out like that, speaks to us of the illumination of the mind and heart and spirit as we humans make our pilgrimage from ignorance to knowledge and understanding. The only element missing from the metaphor of the evaporating mist is the role we humans play in the drama. We are participants in it. To see the morning mist evaporate and reveal a glorious landscape is to participate in the drama emotionally but in no other way. We exult in it, but we do not propel it. In the gaining of knowledge and understanding, however, we are the propellants. Neither comes to us of its own accord. Only continued hard work, guided by the highest standards of accuracy we can establish, brings to us the knowledge we seek and the understanding for which we yearn.

We end then where we began—with ourselves, trying to understand who we are, where we come from, why we are here, where we are going, what it all means, and what we ought to do. We look to our religion to tell us. No other discipline attempts so difficult a task. None can hope to succeed at it. Religion itself cannot. The new paradigm for religion faces this dilemma squarely. Apart from fanaticism, which is a perversion of religion, our faith can do little for us unless it exchanges the old paradigm for the new. This is the conclusion to which inquiry leads. This is the answer to the most basic questions we can ask.

The new paradigm for religion senses urgency within itself. The literature of doom is enormous today and growing. It covers everything from an exploding population that threatens to inundate the earth, to rising world temperatures, and/or to nuclear war. All of these, and many other apocalyptic scenarios, are frightening in their plausibility and terrifying in their possible immediacy. The adoption of a new paradigm for religion will not save the world. Would that it could! A religion centered in ideals, reinforcing the demand that we live by them, would weigh heavily in the balance of hope as against despair.

In the end, life's meaning and purpose for each of us is in what we do with the life each of us is given to live. The purpose of life is not external to us, as the religions in the old paradigm have so long supposed. It is not to be explained by a plan some distant deity has for us. Life's meaning and purpose is to be found in what we choose to do, in what we propose to make of life here and now. Inescapably we are at the center of it all. We are the actors. We do the choosing. That is why, despite the ill-fortune that falls upon us from time to time, we can be called to account. It all comes back to us—back to what we make of life and what we propose to do with it, and why.

There is no cosmic answer to the question of the meaning of my life or of yours either, at least none that we can state and prove. Neither monuments of stone nor scrolls in a library will perpetuate our memory very long. And in any case we are likely to know little about it. What we know is the meaning we find here and now. The meaning we know is in the joy and exultation we find in life, in the here and now; in the good we can do; in the suffering we can alleviate; in the love we share, the love we freely give, and the love that returns to us, often when we have not really earned it.

Notes

1. Bertrand Russell, *Why I Am Not a Christian* (New York: Simon and Schuster, 1964), p. 115.

2. Steven Weinberg, *The First Three Minutes* (New York: Bantam Books, 1977), p. 144.

3. James Trefil, *The Dark Side of the Universe* (New York: Charles Scribner's Sons, 1988), p. 192.

Appendix

John Rawls, Professor of Philosophy at Harvard, established his reputation with *A Theory of Justice* in 1971. The *Nation* said the book was simply without rival. The *New York Times* called it magisterial and the London *Times Literary Supplement* spoke of it as possibly the most notable contribution to English political philosophy since Henry Sidgwick and John Stuart Mill.

In 1993 Rawls published *Political Liberalism*,[1] which is enjoying similar acclaim. In a few terse pages in his introduction he outlines what he believes to be the distinguishing characteristics of political liberalism.

He begins by observing (p. xvi) that democratic society does not enjoy consensus as to the basic principles on which it rests. Liberals, conservatives, moderates, socialists, communists are among the constituent groups to be found in almost any democracy.

Reading these words, religious Liberals will find themselves thinking that the same is true of religious Liberalism. It, too, enjoys no consensus on basic convictions. Humanists, theists, Christians, agnostics, and atheists are all to be found among those who think of themselves as Liberals in religion. The bases of their thought often directly contradict one another.

As a result of their lack of consensus on basics, Rawls continues (p. xix), modern democracies must face the fact of pluralism on religious, philosphical, and moral doctrines. Here again, religious Liberals will find themselves nodding in agreement, for they have long openly championed pluralism in religion. They see it as the only valid way, given the strength of conviction that characterizes religious people.

On what basis, other than that of mutual tolerance, which they, the Liberals, have always advocated, can people of opposing convictions expect to get along with one another? they ask.

Confronting the fact of pluralism in democracies, political liberalism has to ask itself how a society made up of contending and inconsistent beliefs can hold together, Rawls points out. Answering his own question, he replies: (p. xx) "Rather than referring to its political conception of justice as true, political liberalism refers to it as reasonable instead. It is not merely a verbal matter," he continues, "but goes to the heart of the question."

And again, so say the religious Liberals. They, too, do not regard their teachings as true in an absolute sense. In fact, religious Liberals go further and insist that no religious body can claim, as so many do, that its teachings are absolutely true. Instead, the Liberals invite one and all to ponder all religious teachings including their own, and see how far any of them are persuasive.

This approach to the problem of conflicting basic conceptions is not new, Rawls continues (p. xxi). "When moral philosophy began, say with Socrates, ancient religion was a civic religion of public and social practice. [It] was not based on a sacred work like the Bible. . . . The Iliad and the Odyssey were never sacred texts. . . . There was no class of priests who dispensed the necessary means of grace."

As a result, Rawls argues (p. xxii), "In respecting the Homeric ideal . . . Greek philosophy had to work out for itself ideas of the highest good for human life. [In ancient Greece] moral philosophy was always the exercise of free, disciplined reason alone. It was not based on religion, much less on revelation." Here again emphatic, even excited agreement from *religious* Liberals.

Rawls goes on (p. xxiv), "The historical origin of political liberalism (and of liberalism more generally) is the Reformation and its aftermath, the long controversies over religious toleration. . . . Something like the modern understanding of liberty of conscience and freedom of thought began then. As Hegel saw, pluralism made religious liberty possible."

Here yet again what Rawls is saying about political liberalism exactly describes religious Liberalism. Like the ancient Greeks, present-day Liberals in religion recognize no authoritative scriptures or priesthood or tradition. They believe that we humans are on our own.

Unlike the traditionalists in Judaism, Christianity, and Islam, they hold their basic beliefs not as absolute truth, but as reasonable constructions of what the truth might be.

At this point the importance for religious Liberalism of what Rawls is saying about political liberalism becomes clear. Asked what distinguishes them, too many Liberals in religion have been accustomed to list noble principles like freedom of conscience, the objective pursuit of truth, human dignity, human love, and more recently, the importance of the environment. They do this, seemingly unaware of the vast number of people who profess these same ideals, but do not think of themselves as Liberals in religion at all.

Obviously, then, listing all the good things they believe in does not tell the Liberals or anyone else what distinguishes the Liberals and sets them apart from other committed religious people. Too many have supposed that the Liberal task is to assemble new and improved statements of belief. I would argue that they are mistaken. Liberalism in religion is not distinguished by doctrines said to be "liberal." It is distinguished by an open inquiring attitude toward all doctrines, in particular toward those with which they disagree.

Concluding his introduction to *Political Liberalism*, Rawls returns to the question: How is a just society of free and equal citizens possible when its citizens are profoundly divided by reasonable religious, philosophical, and moral doctrines (p. xxv)? This was not a problem in the ancient world, he reminds us. People then "did not know [today's] clash between salvationist, creedal, and expansionist religions. . . . What is new about this clash is that it introduces [into the debate] a transcendent element not admitting of compromise."

It was this very inability to compromise—the inflexibility of the traditional religions in the face of conflicting claims to know truth— that brought the liberal movement in religion into being. To resolve the problem of mutually contradictory "truths" among the religions, Western thinkers "by the eighteenth century were attempting to establish a basis of moral knowledge independent of ecclesiastical authority and available to the ordinary reasonable and conscientious persons," Rawls says (p. xxvi).

Immanuel Kant and David Hume solved the problem by insisting that high motivation toward our fellow creatures resides with us, Rawls adds, but political liberalism leaves the question open. Here, however, religious Liberalism would agree with Kant and Hume that high motivation toward our fellow humans can and will move us toward an ever-increasing operable basis for moral action. Rawls, on his part, does not really leave the question open either, for he goes on to say (p. xxvii) that political liberalism affirms that the moral order arises from ourselves "with respect to a political conception of justice for a constitutional democratic regime."

Religious Liberals have long needed a clearer understanding of themselves. They should read John Rawls on *Political Liberalism.* For me, no book in theology can match its relevance to the question of who the *religious* Liberals are, what they stand for, and why.

Note

1. John Rawls, *Political Liberalism* (New York: Columbia University Press, 1993).

Index